FRONT ROW LADY: STORIES FROM A LIFE

ISBN: 978-0-9971257-4-0

Book and Cover Design by Blue Jay Ink
Ojai, California
bluejayink.com

BLUE JAY INK
Published in the United States by
Blue Jay Ink, 451A East Ojai Avenue, Ojai, CA 90302
bluejayink.com

FRONT ROW LADY: STORIES FROM A LIFE

a memoir by
Kathleen Larronde Hellwitz

BLUE JAY INK
Ojai, California

FRONT ROW LADY: STORIES FROM A LIFE

Table of Contents

Acknowledgments

At the age of eighty-one, I have a lot of life to look back on, and what stands out for me is the abundance of teachers who have crossed my path. Some have been older and wiser, while others have been much younger, with quite unexpected wisdom to share. Some have lectured; others have changed me by example. Some lessons I have learned quickly; others have taken almost a lifetime, but I need to thank one and all for sharing their gifts with me through the decades. Certainly, there are too many to call out by name here, but I think you know who you are. So please accept my sincere gratitude.

* * *

Note: Although the stories are arranged chronologically, I wrote them over a period of several years.

Childhood

The First Day

Well, from what I have been told, I came into this world and within twenty-four hours was bleeding to death. I must have known something wasn't quite right and wanted to check out before I had fully arrived. But a young intern at Hollywood Presbyterian Hospital stepped in and diagnosed my nosebleed as an internal hemorrhage and got three people who had my blood type to donate blood, which was injected into my left fanny.

But I am getting ahead of myself.

It seems that my father had been expecting a boy, and he had already gone and put my name in the cement in the backyard of our house at 12214 Viewcrest Road in Studio City: William George Murphy, III. When Dad saw that I wasn't a boy, he fled the hospital, drove back to the San Fernando Valley, and went to the Zombie Café on Ventura Boulevard in Studio City, where he began to drown his sorrows as only an Irish alcoholic can do. My Uncle Jippy, my mother's brother, joined him there.

Back at the hospital, by the time the intern figured out the true nature of my problem, time was running out for me. Overlaying all this was the need to give me a name—quickly. So they named me after my mother. Thus, my first "first name" was Juanita.

Once everyone realized how sick I was, my Grandma Larronde got in her old Dodge and went to look for my father and her youngest son. She finally found them at the Zombie Café and escorted them back to the hospital, where Dad, my uncle, and the young intern each gave me a pint of their precious blood. I am sure my father and my uncle's blood was pretty well laced with scotch by then. At this point, Dad fell madly in love with me and began singing, "Love Walked In." A complete turnaround.

So that was the first day.

When I lived, thanks to the transfusions, my father insisted on giving me the name Kathleen, despite the fact that there was no saint by that name and the priest who was going to christen me refused to do so unless I was given a saint's name.

Dad said, "Fine. Then we just won't have her christened!" And the priest gave in.

Fred Astaire

My parents met in Blessed Sacrament Grammar School when the teacher placed my mom between two bad boys to keep them from fighting; one of them was my dad. One day years later, my mother went to the Broadway Department Store at Hollywood and Vine to shop, where she met my dad for the second time. He was the floor walker, dressed in a tuxedo-type outfit and looking very handsome.

They started to date. She proposed, or so he said. He was a drinker. Mom was unhappy with that and asked him to quit. He agreed, and they had a dry wedding reception. Soon Mom was with child (me) and Dad started drinking again. She didn't like that at all, so she went home to her mother (her father had died when she was ten) and told her that my father was drinking again and she wanted an annulment.

Grandma Larronde said, "Not if you're with child."

Mother had wanted to be a dancer and dance with Fred Astaire, and she wasn't pleased with how things were going, but she was stuck. In 1937, women didn't have the choices they have today.

From day one, I pretty much knew my mother wasn't pleased with me, although I didn't know why. When I heard this story from my Uncle Jim when I was about in my mid-forties, I felt like so much of my life finally made sense.

My Ruthie

Growing up was not always easy for me. For many years, I couldn't have told you why. I just knew there was something different about me and my life.

Then one day in my forty-fifth year, I was browsing in an antique shop and was drawn to a glass case filled with old dolls. As I approached the case, my body began to shake and my feet stopped moving. My eyes couldn't stop staring at one particular doll in the case. The saleslady saw me and, assuming I was interested, came over to assist me. She had to ask me more than once if there was something I would particularly like to see. Finally, I was able to speak but only barely. I had to point. She understood and opened the case, removed the doll, and placed it in my trembling hands.

I had no idea why I was reacting the way I was. I was so out of control. Tears were rushing down my cheeks and I could hardly breathe. Someone brought a chair for me. As I sat rocking the doll in my arms, I cried out, "Ruthie. My Ruthie."

"Do you want her?" the saleslady asked.

I nodded yes, while managing to get the money out of my purse to pay her. As I did this, pictures began to flash in my mind of my mother standing over me, beating me in my stomach with the head of my Ruthie. I must have been two or three.

This was the beginning of my opening up to remembering and understanding why my early life wasn't easy.

The House I Grew Up In

The house I grew up in was built in 1937, the year before I was born. It is located on a quiet little dead-end street in the foothills of Studio City in the San Fernando Valley. 12214 Viewcrest Road has no sidewalks, and our driveway has a slight slope to it that leads to the first level where my house with its two-car garage sits. At the bottom of the drive is a huge mailbox resting on top of a small retaining wall, with a lovely liquid amber tree planted just behind it. To get to the front door, you walk up a gently winding red brick path bordered by a short box hedge. To the left of the box hedge are Mother's azaleas and some ferns. On the left of the walkway is the house, and on the right is the lawn, bordered on two sides by an ivy bank. A giant blue spruce grows near the far property line, and three birch trees are planted just as you start up the walk.

When you reach the end of the path, the red brick steps leading up to the porch are on your left. The house is considered to be an English Cottage type and is painted a light cream color with brown trim. The roof is steeply pitched with shake shingles. There is a large chimney in the middle of the front of the house, with a large window to the left and a small one to the right. As you enter the front hall, there is a closet immediately to the right and a tall, narrow marble-top table just past it. A mirror hangs over the entry table.

As you stand in the entry, to your left is a small room which changes in use over the years from den, to nursery, to my room. The room has a walk-in closet and a three-quarter bath which leads to the back porch where the wringer washer is located. Past the back porch is the landing where the clothes are hung to dry on a line that runs out over the service yard where the incinerator is. The back of garage opens up to this service yard where there is a slab of concrete with my first name written in the cement: William George Murphy, III.

You go through the back porch into the kitchen. This is Mother's favorite room. She always gets up early to bake and make our breakfasts and lunches. It is the room that gets repainted and remodeled the most. The floor is always being redone: first with light linoleum to make the kitchen brighter, and then with a confetti pattern linoleum because the light one showed too much dirt. But when Mother couldn't see the dirt to clean it, she had the floor changed back to a light color again. This is where we eat all our meals, listen to the radio, talk on the phone, and learn to cook and dance. Off the kitchen is the dining room, which is formal and only used on special occasions. Here the furniture is dark and there is a silver tea service on the sideboard.

To the right of the entry hall is the living room, with a large window on the right where the baby grand sits. There is an extra-large sill in this big window. On the same wall is a very big fireplace—set back so you can walk into it—with a huge opening. There are little tiled seats on both sides of the fireplace, and to the left is a small, deeply recessed window with an equally deep sill. At Christmas, I get to put the nativity scene up in this nook. In the summer, it is an extra cool spot to sit and read and dream. The wall to the left of this area has a window seat which holds the wood box that can be fed from outside. The windows in the living room look out over camellias and violets. The furniture in the room is Barker Brothers' best: wingback chairs and heavily carved wooden frames on the couch and the smaller chairs, all covered in fancy brocade upholstery. The carpet in the living room is dusty rose, with the hardwood showing around the baseboards. We have an RCA Victor Victrola to play our 78 recordings, and a bookshelf built-in at the steps in the corner that lead up to the bedrooms. In the middle of the wall facing the fireplace are glass doors that open on a covered screen porch. Past the porch is a brick patio with a sycamore tree planted in the middle of a tree well. My tree. Given to me by Grandma Larronde to celebrate my birth.

The two steps going up to the bedrooms take you to a small alcove with a door that opens to a hall that branches off to the right and left. Directly across from the alcove door is the door to the master bath, and on the right of that door is a telephone nook with a built-in desk, a stool, and the other dial phone in the house. Black is your only color choice for telephones.

To the right of the telephone nook is the children's room, with two closets, both walk-in, and one large enough to hold a dresser. At first the room holds a crib and a dresser. Then a bed is added. Ultimately the crib goes to the basement just outside this room and below the living room, and is replaced by a second Hollywood bed.

To the left of the master bath is a hall, with the linen closet on the right and a glass door on the left leading out to the patio. The master bedroom is at the end of the hall. In there is more dark furniture: a modified four-poster double bed, a highboy with a mirror for Dad, and a shorter dresser with a mirror for Mom. Dad's closet is in the far corner of the room, and next to it is an alcove with Mother's desk, where she pays the bills. Next there is a small room where Mother's dressing table is built-in and her closet is located. A door from this room leads to the master bath, with lots of green tile and shiny water lily wallpaper. The toilet is in an alcove, and there is a full tub and separate shower.

Roly-Poly Chocolate

Before I was born, my parents had a Great Dane named Fritzie. She was a show dog for a while and earned lots of blue ribbons. Those blue ribbons didn't come cheap, though, and pretty soon she became more valuable as a breading bitch. Her pups went for a nice price, most of which was used to pay the food bill for dear Fritzie.

Then I came along and added to the cost of living at 12214 Viewcrest Road. As I began to grow, naturally I was allowed more time in the yard. And typical child that I was, everything I saw I picked up and put in my mouth. Some things were good, others not so much.

One thing, though, really captured my attention and became a major focus of my adventures in the yard. This great find was what I call a roly-poly bug or a pill bug. A roly-poly is a tiny grey bug with a gazillion tiny legs. It scurries along, attracting your attention first. When you touch it, it rolls into a protective ball. A child's wonder. *Wow! What happened*? Then the bug starts walking again. Touch it, it becomes a ball again. This was a game even Mattel couldn't match.

Then my tiny fingers found that I could pick up the little bug when it was a ball. If I laid it on my hand, it opened to walk, and all those little legs tickled my palm. *Wow! Again.* Of course, the next step was to put it in my mouth and taste. *Crunch. Chocolate. Let's do it again.* And I did.

When Mother saw this, she flipped. She took me to the

doctor, who told her that obviously I wasn't getting enough protein in my diet. So my parents took a look at the food costs and realized that, sure enough, because Fritzie was getting fed so well for her pups, the family had been getting less to eat. The decision was made to let Fritzie go to a walnut rancher with a very nice place in the West Valley. According to the story told over the years, I then stopped eating pill bugs, and Mother no longer felt she was depriving her family of necessary nourishment. Dad liked to remember this chapter in our lives at family gatherings. It would always make Mother say, "Oh, Bill! Must you?" He loved getting a rise out of her.

As for me, I can still remember the feeling of those tiny little feet on the palm of my hand. The taste of chocolate? Not so much.

Green Beans

When I was about three or four years old, before my sister was born, I had a difference of opinion with my parents over green beans, and decided to run away from home. I packed my bag with my jammies and took my Ruthie Doll and set out for the neighbors. I first went next door to the Lanams' house and asked if I could stay with them. They said they really didn't have room, and I said I'd just need a pillow and a blanket and I could sleep on the couch. They were sorry but they had no extra pillows. The same was true for the next neighbors, the Levins. So I decided to be brave and break the rule about not crossing the street and go over to the Gards. They too had no extra pillows. And I could not sleep without a pillow. So, in defeat, I returned home, declaring that the next time I ran away from home I'd take my own pillow.

It wasn't till years later that I learned that my parents had called all the neighbors and apprised them of my need for a pillow for sleeping and asked them to let me know no pillows were available.

Three Times a First-Timer

My dad was a traveling salesman. In 1940 when I was two years old, Dad was on a trip in the Midwest when he had an auto accident and broke his right femur. It happened on a country road when he was trying to pass a slow farmer's truck. After the accident, the farmer kindly pulled Dad out of his wrecked car and shoved him into the flatbed of his truck to take him to the hospital. While doing this, though, the farmer compounded Dad's fracture. The hospital they went to in Twin Cities, Minneapolis/St. Paul was not very modern. Dad called Mother to come get him, so she and Uncle John flew back there, and I was left behind to stay with Grandma Larronde.

Dad wanted surgery right away, despite a doctor friend's advice that he should return to UCLA first, where the care was better. Dad persuaded the hospital in the Twin Cities to operate on him immediately. This proved to be a seriously bad choice because fertilizer from the back of the farmer's truck had gotten into Dad's open wound. An infection resulted, which the ill-equipped hospital was not able to find and treat. By the time he finally got back to UCLA, he had a serious case of osteomyelitis, an infection of the bone. He became one of the very first people in the country to be treated with penicillin. After having surgery, he was transferred to the Good Samaritan Hospital in Los Angeles for long-term recovery.

Dad spent weeks in traction in a hospital bed in the

industrial ward at the Good Samaritan, and Mother spent hours in his room. I entertained myself by playing with the hospital wheelchairs. Made of wood with high wicker backs and wicker seats, they creaked when you sat in them. The wheels were almost as tall as I was when I was three. I especially enjoyed putting my Ruthie doll in one and pushing her up and down the hall, and I liked being taken around in one of them myself. Next to the nurses' desk was a small room where they sharpened the hypodermic needles to use on the next patient.

Dad finally came home, but he had to stay in a hospital bed in traction and be attended by nurses. He learned to walk, and eventually was able to go back to work. That's when he became one of the first people in the country to own and drive a car with an automatic transmission. Since he couldn't use his right leg at the time (it was in a brace), he would sit sideways in the front seat and use his left foot for the gas and the brake. You might say his Irish luck put him in the right place at the right time for both penicillin and the automatic transmission.

For the next fifteen years or so, Dad was able to keep his bad leg, with numerous surgeries and medications. Then, at a Christmas party in the late '50s, he was dancing and his partner lost her balance. When he caught her, his femur—after all those surgeries—wasn't strong enough to hold, and it broke like a piece of chalk. The break wasn't jagged, so the two smooth bone ends had nowhere to latch on and knit together, and he had to have his leg amputated above the knee.

This is where his Irish luck kicked in for the third time. Up until then, amputees had to wear a bulky harness, and swing their wooden leg out to move forward. But there was a man in San Clemente who worked with hydraulic devices, and he made one small enough to place in the knee of an artificial leg, which made it look much more natural. So all Dad had to do was shift his weight from right to left, and his right foot would automatically swing forward. This made walking look much less awkward. But you couldn't stand in front of him when he shifted his weight or you'd take the toe of his shoe right in your shin.

Here again, he was one of the first in the country to use this new kind of prosthesis. He went with the inventor to Washington, D. C., to demo it to Congress. We'll never know what other things he might have gotten to be the first to use because he died at forty-nine in 1961.

World War II

World War II started on September 1, 1939, eighty years ago. I was one year old. It began in Germany and ended there on May 8, 1945. The fighting in the Pacific Theater began in 1941 and ended in 1945, when I was seven. At the time, there was one radio show with a host named Gabriel Heatter, whose opening line was: "There is good news tonight." I only remember hearing his show at Grandmother Larronde's house in Hollywood, not at my house. If we got the paper, I didn't read it, and there was no TV. So unlike kids who saw TV news about Vietnam or the Iraq War daily in their living room, my living room was for play. I was definitely quite a sheltered child then.

What I did know was what directly affected me. When the war started, Dad was I-A: ready and fit for military service. A year later, he had his bad auto accident that landed him in a hospital bed in traction for a broken leg. That changed his draft classification to IV-F: physically, mentally, or morally unfit for battle. So he went to work for Camlock, making airplane parts for the war effort, and wearing a uniform of a light tan cotton shirt and pants from Sears, like everyone else who couldn't join in the fight overseas but was doing their part at home.

During the war, we had blackout curtains on our windows. House lights were on sparsely at night, if at all. Cars had their headlights painted black on top, and driving at night was for emergency trips only. When I was four, Dad drove Mother to the hospital in the daytime when she was pregnant and due to deliver my sister. Sugar, coffee, meats, and eggs were rationed so the troops could be fed. My parents bought savings bonds for the war effort. We saved fat, string, and aluminum, even scraping the foil off gum wrappers and rolling it in a ball, and we planted Victory Gardens at my house and Grandma Larronde's.

Since the Japanese army was spying in submarines off the coast, oceanfront property was almost being given away during that time. Both my uncles bought Malibu beachfront land and built homes where they lived for the rest of their lives. The big searchlights originally used to spot enemy aircraft in the war ultimately were best known for their use in advertising. They were used to attract people: a new movie, a new shopping center, a new anything. The searchlights' connection to the war soon faded in the economic boom that followed.

My mother's two brothers served in the war. Uncle John was in the infantry in the European Theater, and Uncle Jimmy was a pilot who flew missions in the Pacific Theater. Uncle Jimmy brought home lots of souvenirs from places like Java—pretty fabrics and a bamboo cane—and Uncle John brought home "real" Dutch wooden shoes. I still have the cane and use it from time to time, but not the shoes.

Uncle Jimmy was lost at sea in the South Pacific several times, once with Louie Zamperini, author of the bestselling autobiography Unbroken that was later made into a film directed by Angelina Jolie. When my uncle's plane crashed into the Pacific, it was assumed he'd died. So when he was found alive the first time, both my mother and grandmother cried for joy. This was the first but not the last time I would see someone cry for happiness, not pain or sorrow. Tears were always a bad thing for me, especially since I was told not to cry or I'd be given something to cry about.

Grandma Larronde's House

When my father had his accident out of state, my mother and uncle went to get him. I was taken to Grandma Larronde's house at 1844 North Kingsley Drive in Hollywood where I stayed for a very long time. Her house was wonderfully different from mine. I had so much freedom there. I was two years old and now I could go to the bathroom whenever I needed. In the mornings, I could get out of my bed and climb in with Grandmother. She was so warm and she would let me put my cold feet between her thighs. She would take walks with me. We would cook together, and I had a toy cupboard in the breakfast room.

We had lunches on the terrace underneath the wisteria vine dripping purple flowers and bees coming for the nectar. To purify the water we drank, Grandma used an *oya*, a very large piece of rock with a natural indentation fashioned into a big bowl. You turned on the faucet above, and let the water fill the bowl and seep through the big porous rock into a pitcher below. The water was so cool and clean.

I would dress up and play "fashion show" on the terrace. Grandmother and Great Aunt Ethel, her sister, would ask me questions about the outfits I was wearing: How much did that cost? What material is it? What sizes is it available in? It was so grown-up and fun. Both Gram and Great Aunt Ethel made clothes for me, and Aunt Ethel would make matching clothes for my Ruthie Doll. My mother couldn't sew, so I learned how to sew from Great Aunt Ethel and Aunt Mabel, my dad's sister.

Great Aunt Ethel had her own set of rooms at Grandmother's house. I loved the smell of her cold cream. I loved lying in her bed with her on her screened porch and learning to count in Spanish, German, and French. We would make tea on that porch and play makeup at her dressing table. Once I tried to learn to strike a match on her coffee table and accidently set the area rug on fire. I do not remember being punished. It was a lesson.

In the backyard Grandma had an aviary covered with ivy. First you went into the little anteroom and closed the door behind you. Then you could open the door to the big cage to feed and give fresh water to the beautiful canaries. Near the aviary was a big fishpond, with a huge growth of bamboo and water lilies at one end—a perfect home for the happy koi who lived there.

Next to the fishpond was a Meyers sweet lime tree, and we would always have fresh limeade made from that wonderful fruit. Way in the back Grandma had a World War II Victory Garden with rhubarb, all kinds of vegetables, melons, and berries. Behind the garden was a shed where my uncles fixed and built things. Several huge avocado trees grew in the yard, and under one was a big picnic table and a stone wood-burning cook stove. We would have meals out there often. I can still taste the watermelon. Grandmother loved carnations and had a bed exclusively for them by the back door.

Her house had a wonderful wide porch in front, with a swing that looked out over a very tall flagpole in the front yard. The avocado tree there made a wonderful fort because it had big branches that were partly horizontal, so you could lie on them and lean back against the trunk. It was such a friendly tree. There was a parkway in front of her house that ran all up and down the street. Up the street was a Frank Lloyd Wright home, and down the street was the El Adobe Market, which had a radio station on the second floor that played popular music. Was it Al Jarvis, the radio announcer with the make-believe ballroom? Or was it Peter Potter spinning the Platters?

One time after we had been shopping, Grandma opened the car door to remove the grocery bags. One bag fell out and liquor bottles broke all over the driveway. I remember another time when she left the Dodge in the driveway, filled with Christmas presents and the keys still in the ignition, and the car was stolen. It was recovered later, with little, if any, damage.

Grandma had long grey hair with a white streak coming off her forehead. She was a great cook who made her own salad dressing and wonderful stews and roasts. There was always a soup pot going on the stove, especially in the winter. For the holidays, she would make plum pudding and then ladle brandy over it and light it. We would watch the alcohol burn off, with the blue flame dripping off the ladle as she poured the fluid over the pudding. Sometimes I would get under the big dining room table after meals and go around and tickle everyone's ankles. That was a fun game.

My Uncle Jippy taught me to play the piano on Grandma's piano. He and Great Aunt Ethel both played, as did my mother. I learned the first few bars of Beethoven's "Fur Elise," which I still love.

Grandmother and Aunt Ethel liked things from China and they had a mah-jongg game. We never played the game, but I liked to set up the pieces in a long, curved line and then push the last piece and watch all the others fall in turn. We would listen to Walter Winchell on the radio. His opening had something that ended with "and all the ships at sea."

The basement at Grandma's house was full of wonderful things. My uncles developed their film in the darkroom down there. There were tons of old *National Geographics* and lots of dishes. Grandma's house also had a sleeping porch on the second story that wrapped around the back and side of the house that held four to six beds. On one wall hung a print called "September Morn," a racy drawing of a young nude woman about to bathe in a stream—a Marilyn before Marilyn.

My grandfather Pedro Domingo Larronde had died when my mother was just ten, and when I was a child Grandma Larronde had a boyfriend we called Uncle Tom. He was from Canada and was her bridge partner. Aunt Ethel had a boyfriend too, a French perfume maker named Mirto. Uncle Tom was always around, but he had his own place. He used to get us See's Candies every holiday, and he taught my sister and me how to ice skate.

Gramma Larronde died at age sixty-four. I must have been about twelve or so. I really missed her. But when I had asked her about death earlier, she told me that when a person dies and they are thought of each day afterwards, then they really haven't died. I tried to think of her every day, so she would live.

Bird Medicine

Grandma Larronde approached health issues like Peter Rabbit's mother, telling me to get plenty of rest, drink some chamomile tea, and have some toast. She walked every day, especially after meals. We had walking sticks and wore hats when it was sunny. Much of the food she served she grew in her backyard. It was fun staying at her house. She used something she called "bird medicine" for cuts and scrapes, telling me that if the birds used it, it was safe for children. Of course I believed her. She would put BFI Antiseptic Powder on all "owies," and they would be well in no time without drama or tears or Band-Aids.

When I moved from Gram's house back to my parents' home, I was surrounded by the allopathic mode of medicine used by the doctors who were treating my father's broken and infected leg. Our house had nurses with routines, special diets, and meds, all geared to getting Dad well. Mother had a pill for everything and was always offering them to those in need; aspirin was her favorite. In time, she had all the females in the house on iron and thyroid supplements. Dad was the only one allowed real pain meds, and then he discovered Christian Science and kicked the morphine they'd had him on in the hospital.

If I had a headache or female cramp, Dad would threaten to take me to the hospital for an operation if I didn't deal with it, which meant "shut up." When my tonsils were removed, he was very supportive initially. But I sure couldn't milk it for long. After my wisdom teeth were pulled, I was given a package of gum and told to chew it all to prevent dry sockets. Within three days we all attended a roast beef feast at a friend's house, and I was able to eat everything without any pain.

Later on, Gram found a new favorite piece of advice: "Don't be a fool and pay the doctor to give you direction and then ignore it. You're just wasting your money then." I'm not sure who this advice was directed at, but she said it a lot.

Perfume

I have some vague memories of my parents arguing in the kitchen, with me grabbing at their knees and crying.

There are longer memories of my dad in the living room at night, drinking and talking with friends and telling jokes. I am in my room and have to go to the bathroom, but I have been put to bed and cannot get up without the risk of being spanked. I get up anyway, and on my way back from the bathroom, I slip behind the door in the hall off the living room just to listen for a minute. Instead, I fall asleep. When I am discovered by my parents, they are furious with me for disobeying them, and they give me a good spanking.

I remember being in bed, sick with the mumps, and again being told not to get out of bed for any reason. I had some perfume by my bed and I drank it. Of course it tasted awful, and I needed to wash my mouth out but couldn't without permission. My mother was in the kitchen, way across the house, and no matter how loudly I called, she did not hear me. So I decided to spit out the window. That decision led me to open the screen to be able to spit on the ground, but I fell out and landed headfirst on the ground along with the spittle. I couldn't get back up into my room and into my bed, so I had to go around the back and knock on the kitchen door to get my mother's attention. She was on the phone and very surprised to see me at the door. I think the knot on my forehead saved me from being punished.

Another time Mother dressed me up and sent me into the backyard to play. Then she locked all the doors and got on the phone. I was playing by myself, and realized I needed to move my bowels. I had had my chance earlier to go but couldn't. So when I knocked on the door to get into the bathroom, my mother continued to talk on the phone and ignored me. Naturally, I went in my pants and when she came and found me crying, I got punished for messing my pants.

We had a fairytale map in our room behind the door, and it was great fun running our fingers along the trail from the lowlands to the castle. Mother would come in and wake me up for school. When I didn't rise in the time she thought I should, she would pour cold water on me.

Nudity was common. We swam in the nude and were nude in the bath with both parents.

I remember my parents having friends over for cocktails and then going out to dinner, leaving the unfinished drinks on the coffee table in the living room. I remember finishing off those drinks.

Dad's Joke

My father loved to tease people, especially his mother. Grandmother Murphy had given him some advice on his wedding day that he found laughable. She told him, "Don't let your wife ever see you nude, and don't have intercourse more than once a week." He vowed to pay her back one day.

His response came several years later. When I was about two or three, Dad taught me that the word "modest" meant I should remove all my clothes and take an air bath like Gramma Larronde had taught me to do when she babysat.

He knew that when his mother was the babysitter, her first words to me would be, "Now you be a modest young lady." Sure enough, she would say those words and I would strip and dance about, much to my dad's delight and his mother's horror. As for me? I loved any excuse to be a "Nicky Nudist."

The Larronde House on Bunker Hill

On Sundays when I was very young, I would go with my family on drives to visit with various relatives both near and far. Dad's mother and sister lived about a mile away, Mom's mother and her sister lived about ten miles from us, and Mom's father's sisters lived twenty-five miles away in in a fabulous Victorian mansion on Bunker Hill in downtown LA.

Mom's father had three sisters who never married and lived together till they died; Madeleine, Marianna, and Caroline were well known on the Wall Street of Los Angeles as the guardians of the Larronde/Etchemendy millions. Their mother, my great grandmother Juana, had originally married Jean Etchemendy, a Basque sheepherder, and together they had three children. When Jean died, Juana married his best friend, Pierre Larronde, another sheepherder from the same area in the Pyrenees, and they had three children.

Jean Etchemendy and Pierre Larronde were best friends who had moved from Spain to South America to do some gold mining, before they came to California to join the gold rush. There were no taxes at the time, and the men were frugal. They quickly began to amass a fortune and hang around with people like the Dohenys. My grandfather Pedro Domingo Larronde, one of my great grandmother's six children, was a principal in The Franco American Baking Company in LA.

Mom's three aunts, who had no children of their own, were quite astute, and they invested wisely in the stock market where they made a huge amount of money. Two of the aunts, Marianna and Madeleine, later adopted four Chinese girls who had been orphaned when their parents, who worked for the family, died.

I loved going to that house. The mansion was full of old,

overstuffed, dark wood furniture covered in velvet the color of red wine. The dark red drapes were always drawn tight, which kept the interior of the house dark. The adults drank sherry and the children were allowed soft drinks. The Chinese girls would take me and my sister upstairs to the turret on the fourth floor. The carpets were thick and dark, and they muffled the sounds of us giggling upstairs, away from the grown-ups.

The kitchen was accessible from the back of the house and was in stark contrast to the living quarters upstairs in that it had a floor of shiny cream-colored tile, and not a sign of fabric or dark wood anywhere. At Christmas time this was where the cook made sweet tamales for everyone.

* * *

When the ladies from Bunker Hill came to our house for tea, they were driven by a chauffeur named Bruce. He sat in the car the whole time they were there. We would be in the living room having tea and whatever dessert Mother made that day. And I would be worried about Bruce.

I would ask, "Isn't he hungry? Does he want something to eat?"

And with each question I was told no, no, and more nos. I didn't believe them and would slip away, supposedly to use the restroom. Instead, I would go to the kitchen where our maid Harriet was serving and ask her for a plate of food for the chauffeur. I would then take it out the back door, down the steps, through the gate, and out to the driveway where I would hand it to Bruce, who happily inhaled every morsel. Bruce and his wife and I exchanged Christmas cards until he passed away, and I was probably forty years old by then.

Today Bunker Hill is covered with structures that house

the Dorothy Chandler Pavilion, the Cathedral of Our Lady of the Angels, and, of course, lots of parking lots.

Siblings

I have two siblings, both sisters. Suzanne is four years my junior, Christina eleven. Because of our age difference, Chrisy is the one I mothered. When she was a baby her changing table was in the den, soon to be my room. I changed her diapers and even threw away the dried-up end of her umbilical cord. Mother was detached from me and Chrisy but not from Suzanne.

Famous

I wanted to be famous since before I can remember. I grew up in Studio City, California, surrounded by famous people year-round. My mother was insane for movie stars. To her, movie stars meant famous, famous meant movie stars.

Our garden was filled with clippings and slips she had taken after dark from the yards of our famous neighbors.

One time Mother pulled a U-turn in the middle of Ventura Blvd to follow Clark Gable home to get his autograph. After a great deal of research, my mother tracked down and hired Clark Gable's maid. She actually turned out to be quite lovely. Dear Harriet was with us for decades.

My mother often confided that her deepest desire was to dance off into the sunset with Fred Astaire.

My neighborhood was wall-to-wall movie stars. We had Audie Murphy, Mickey Rooney, and Donald O'Connor. We had

Rhys Williams and George Chandler, along with regular James Dean sightings as he raced his car to and from his friend's house. Oh, and my very favorite: dear Dick Elliot with his little wiener dog. They were both so round and pleasant and fun to chat with when we took walks together.

What was really fun was to see them on TV at night, knowing they were really right next door.

Oh, and our neighbor Leon Ames not only acted in movies and on stage, he also owned the local Ford dealership. He was so famous he got kidnapped, stuffed in the trunk of his car, and held for ransom, making him the lead story on the nightly news till he was found alive several days later.

Oh, how I longed to be famous too! But my mother's answer was always, "NO."

Interwoven with famous people through carpools, school carnivals, pool parties, and Halloween. Bound by casseroles that make a neighborhood in good times and bad.

Even my house got a screen test and was in a movie. The day of the shoot every kid on the block stayed home from school to watch the actors, the cameras, the lights, and the dozens of people milling about. But not me or my sister. We had to go to school. My own house in a movie, and I couldn't even watch.

I was so close to famous, I could almost have had it for breakfast. Almost.

We ate out a lot, and we always went to restaurants frequented by stars: John Wayne, Gordon McCrae, Liz Taylor—oh, the list was endless. One time, Jackie Cooper approached my parents to ask if they would bring me in for a screen test. My heart fluttered, my face flushed, and my stomach dropped to the floor.

And then, very politely, my mother said, "No."

Brushes with "my big break" would happen regularly over the years, but however much my mother loved movie stars, her answer would forever and always be "No."

"Would your daughter like to be on the Barbara Ann Bread billboard?"

Mother: "No."

"Would your daughter like to play Grace Kelly as a young girl?"

Mother: "No."

"We're looking for a young girl to ..."

Mother: "No."

My mother would offer explanations like how she'd heard that Natalie Wood was rude to a saleslady, and that she didn't want me turning out that way. There were other explanations, but that was her fallback.

As I recall the stories, it seems that my mother and father used to go to Monty's Steak House out on Ventura Boulevard in the Encino area or maybe a little farther out. In those days Ventura Boulevard was sparsely populated, and this restaurant would have been considered a roadhouse. My father loved his steak blood rare. Anyway, I must have been all of two or so, and there was an actor of some note named Dennis Morgan who liked to frequent the same steak house. Dennis was dressed in his World War II uniform, and I was attracted to him because in my eyes he was my Uncle Jippy, my mother's brother Jim, who was a pilot in the Air Force. Somehow this attraction led to some conversation, and Dennis was going to be making a new movie soon and wondered if my parents would allow me to be in that movie with him.

"NO!!!" was my mother's response.

It's hard to know why Mother always said no, but she had desperately wanted to be a dancer, and she'd married a drinker instead. Things got complicated—and then I came along. Somewhere in there, I think I got in between her and her dream of dancing off into the sunset with Fred. I think "No" was easier than "I wish you weren't here."

High school graduation led to college, and college led to jobs and husbands and relocating regularly, and the years flew by. And although fame continued to surround me, it also continued to elude me. But now I had kids, and somehow fame didn't seem to matter so much. There were classes they wanted to take and things they want to be when they grew up, so I started to address my mother's NOES by saying "YES" whenever I could. YES to art class, YES to swimming lessons, YES to cheerleading camp, soccer teams, lessons, trips, classes. Yes. Yes. Yes.

YES turned out to be more fun than I anticipated. So when my kids left home, I started saying YES to other kids. Donating to arts organizations that give kids a voice. Those YESES led to me taking up residency in the front row of a little hole-in-the-wall theater to witness those young voices take flight. I ended up liking the front row so much I stayed to watch all the other voices of that little theater come to life. Plays and concerts and poetry— they called it "theater in your lap"—and I went there a lot. The front row of Theater 150 became my second home.

Smiles of Harriet

Once my mother found out where Clark Gable lived, she made frequent trips past his place, until one day she spotted his housekeeper getting in her car and stopped to have a chat.

Eventually dear Harriet became our maid too. She was

with us for many years. I remember about a decade into her time with us when she was dusting in the living room, and I noticed that her right cheek had a really bad burn scar. When I asked her how long she'd had the scar, she said since she was burned by some hot coffee when she was very young. I was amazed. I had known her for ten years and never seen it before.

When I asked her why she thought I hadn't I seen the scar before, she said that from the very beginning her mother had told her, "No one will ever notice as long as you keep smiling." And sure enough, Harriet was always smiling and giggling, all while she kept cleaning, ironing, and making scratch cookies, biscuits, and her famous monkey bread. I will never forget her.

Indians

I am from the land of the Indians. At least that's what I assume since when I was a little girl and did anything wrong, my father would threaten to send me back to the Indians. This would make me cry to the point that I could not stop, and then he'd say, "Stop or I will give you something to cry about."

This, of course, was the threat of a beating, which I wanted no part of. So I would make a very serious effort to stop crying. I wasn't always successful, especially if I got into the dry gasping phase. My dad was an alcoholic and his mood could change on a dime, so I was never quite sure what he'd do. Sometimes he'd hit me and others he'd hug me. Maybe I would have been better off with the Indians.

Dad's Favorite Story

There was a gas station on top of a hill on the main road between two towns. One day the owner and his son were seated out front when a car coming from the town to their left pulled in to fill up. While the son washed the windows, the driver asked the father what it was like in the town up ahead.

The father replied with his own question: "How was it back where you lived?"

"Awful!" said the driver. "Just awful! I'm so glad to be out of there!"

The father said, "Sadly, you'll probably find the town up ahead just about the same."

The driver huffed, paid up, and drove off quickly, leaving a cloud of dust behind him.

In a few minutes another car coming from the same direction pulled in to get gas. As the son washed the windows and the father pumped the gas, the driver asked what it was like in the town up ahead.

To which the father responded with his question: "How was it back where you lived?"

"Oh! It was so lovely!" the man said. "I just didn't want to leave. But I got a better job!"

"Well," replied the father, "I think you'll find the town up ahead just as lovely, if not more so."

The driver smiled, paid for the gas, and safely pulled out onto the main road.

The son quickly went and sat next to his father. "Dad, both those men asked you the same question about the same town, but you gave them such different answers. Why?"

"Well, son, each man gave me a different answer to my

question, and I've learned over the years that most people will find pretty much what they have left behind because they take themselves with them. It's not where you are, it's who you are. You make the difference."

The Ice Queen

We called my mother the Ice Queen.

When my sister Suzanne and I were old enough to be curious about how we got here, we asked her. Mother took out a book called *Being Born* and showed us a picture in the front: a solid black page with a white dot in the middle. Under the picture it read: "This is how we all began."

Wow! Our interest was certainly piqued!

So we asked just how we got from that dot to us.

She closed the book. "Go ask your father."

Thus our sex education was taken over by an Irish alcoholic who fancied himself quite the ladies' man and needed to tell us all his stories about his conquests, but who wanted his daughters to be virgins when they married.

Which is why MY sex ed became a learning-by-doing experience.

Japanese

I was born in 1938, and in my early years, there was a grocery store in our neighborhood owned by a Japanese family. We had a Japanese housekeeper and gardener; Kiko was our house girl and her brother, whose name I can't remember, was our gardener. Since my father was a traveling salesman, dinner was not a formal occasion at our house. Kiko was responsible for cooking dinner and feeding the kids. Since she was always running around and taking care of the house, my sister and I would be left alone in the kitchen. We would quickly tuck any food we didn't like into our cloth napkins and throw it out in the sink. When we got a garbage disposal, we used that to grind up all the evidence, and Kiko never caught us.

The Japanese grocery store was so much fun for me. The mom worked the register, the dad stocked the shelves, and his brother ran the meat department. The fresh fruits and vegetables were handled by a very old man, who was probably the father of one of the owners. The old man was so kind to me. He always gave me fresh peas in the pod to chew on while Mother was shopping. I can still taste their sweet juicy flavor. I much prefer raw peas in the pod to cooked.

One day when I was probably about four, no one came to work. Our house had no gardener and no caregiver, and the grocery store was closed. Everyone was gone. They disappeared without a trace. It wasn't until years later that I learned why. I was not happy then. I am not now. I'm outraged about the way we treated the Japanese.

The Radio

We had a small radio on the window shelf in the kitchen breakfast nook in the house where I grew up. In the morning while we had our fresh-squeezed OJ and oatmeal, we would listen to *The Breakfast Club*, and Mother would teach us how to do the Box Step, the Charleston, or whatever dance step went with the music playing. At dinnertime we would listen to *The Lone Ranger*, *The Whistler*, *The Bob Hope Show*, *The*

Burns and Allen Show, or *The Lux Radio Theater*. On warm days we would open the kitchen window, turn the radio to face the backyard, and let whoever was gardening, playing, or sunbathing listen to the ball game, the soaps, or game shows like *Truth or Consequences* and *Stop the Music*.

In the living room we had a large console with another radio and an RCA Victrola for playing our 78 records. Here the grown-ups listened to the president speak and followed the baseball and football games and the boxing matches. I enjoyed my special 78s for kids—Nat King Cole's children's music, especially the song "Kee-Mo Ky-Mo," Irene Dunn reading "The Littlest Angel," and the fairytale "The Twelve Dancing Princesses."

Dad had a friend who worked for RCA, pressing records, who would bring outtakes from Bing Crosby's recording sessions, bloopers and all, and play them for the grown-ups after we kids were in bed.

My sister and I had a smaller radio in our bedroom where we would listen to soap operas when we were home from school or sick in bed. On Saturday mornings we'd listen to the children's show *Let's Pretend*. Sometimes on special occasions we were allowed to listen as we fell asleep to *Gun Smoke*, *Amos 'n' Andy*, *Fibber McGee and Molly*, *The Great Gildersleeve*, or *Abbott & Costello*. The choices were endless and always kept our imagination busy. It was like having someone read to us. I would close my eyes and see the pictures in my mind. I loved radios wherever they were: in the house or car, at the beach or by the pool.

My memories of those programs and the 78 records are ever so much more vivid than all the TV shows I have ever seen. TV does all the work for you. Radio and records created an inviting place to go and use your imagination. You were part of the presentation. You had to be an active listener for radio to work. I loved it then and still do.

The Beach House

Grandma Larronde had a beach cabin in Malibu with a sign that read: "The Three J's" for her three children: Juanita, John, and Jim.

When we would first arrive at the beach cabin at the beginning of summer, the path dug out of the hillside would be overgrown with castor bean and other chaparral. Our first chore was to clear the path. Then for the next two or three months while we stayed there, the path would remain clear due to daily use.

The cabin had no hot water and the bathroom was outside in a breezeway between the house and the garage; there was no door or wall at either end of this hallway. The toilet was in one closet-like place and the shower in another. Castor bean plants grew all around the house, and the back yard was made of packed dirt. Inside the cabin, there was sand on the wooden floors which were painted grey.

The kitchen had a big gas stove, with a sink on the right with a window that overlooked a dirt road, and an icebox on the left. There was a drain in the floor so the melt-down from the ice could drop directly onto the dirt below. We'd walk with one of our uncles to the icehouse up the way to get blocks of ice to keep our food cold, and we'd bring them home in a small red wagon.

In the living room was a couch, some wicker chairs, a big stone fireplace which was the main source of heat for the house, and a large library table that always had a pack of playing cards in the drawer. The lamp on the fireplace mantle must have come from a bar because when you lit it, the light bulb warmed up a picture of a boy who began to move, and then you could see him peeing into a river. Above his picture it said: "Why you should never drink water." My dad would sit on the couch after dinner, smoking his pipe. There was a slot machine in the living room, and my sister and I believed that Dad's pipe could make nickels. He would do some hocus-po-cus with the pipe, and there would be nickels in his hand. It made for a fun game for us, and our cousins and friends.

To the back of the house there was a closed-in porch area that held the dining room table, long like a picnic table, where we ate as a family. Windows ran all along the back wall. Under them were daybeds that were used as couches in the day and for sleeping at night. Two bedrooms were off the living room, with the kitchen in between them. My parents' bedroom had a wash basin in the corner, a closet of sorts, and a Murphy bed in the wall which was kept closed up in the daytime. I am told that my first sister was conceived in that Murphy bed in the single bedroom in the cabin at the beach.

To the left of the living room was the kids' sleeping area, which was divided into two parts with a window at each end; one window looked into the dining area and the other looked out over the dirt road that ran in front of the house. At night, lights from the trucks and cars that traveled the Pacific Coast Highway would shine through the front window, and move across the walls and over the cots. In our room we had a wash basin and a white enamel commode that we kept tucked under our cots to use at night.

When I was a child sleeping in that room, one night I had a vision of a mountain lion through the front window. The crea-ture was brilliant with light and color, and very real. When I told my family about it the next morning they told me I must have been dreaming. I can still feel the wooden floor beneath my bare feet as I stood and saw this beautiful vision. I can still feel the awesome power I felt then. I don't believe I was dreaming.

* * *

My father and uncles used to go skin diving across the PCH off the point at Topanga, and we would have the fresh abalone, perch, rock cod, and lobster they caught. Gram would keep the lobsters in the shower stall before they were cooked. We had an old tin tub that we bathed in. Grandma would put the tin in the shower and boil hot water for our baths. It was scary to get in and out of the tin tub with live lobsters crawling around. We knew that after Grandma boiled the hot water for our bath, she would start boiling a fresh pot of water to cook the lobsters.

When my uncles and father caught abalone, they would take it to the backyard to a pounding block made from an old tree stump. They would cut the muscle out of the shell and trim the sides before slicing the muscle into thin pieces to be pounded for Gram. She would bread the slices and fry them in butter for dinner, adding a squeeze of fresh lemon on top. The intestinal remains in the shells were left for me to go through in search of abalone pearls, which I often found. I can still feel the soft yet strong intestines between my fingers as I felt around for those pearls. Such a slimy search, but what a great reward it was to run into something hard, no matter the size. Then we had to cut the sack and remove the treasure. Yuck!

One night when we were eating dinner, everyone was served a lobster but me. I complained to my father that I wanted one too. He told me I didn't like lobster. I said I did, although I'd never had any before. I just felt left out and wanted to belong to the family. Instead of giving me a trial taste, Dad went to the kitchen and got an especially small lobster and put it on my plate. Naturally, my young taste buds were not ready for this experience, and I soon discovered that I did not like lobster. But my father made me sit there at the table and go without dessert for a long time after everyone else had gotten up from the table, to make his point that he was right. I think my grand-mother finally rescued me, but I had to go straight to bed. I felt such shame from this experience. I will never forget it. It was cruel but not unusual behavior for my father, who drank heavily.

* * *

Grandma's boyfriend, we called him Uncle Tom, was a frequent guest at the beach house, and he would help us sweep the floors at the end of each day. He would also go with us to the gully behind the cabin. Once we'd reach the floor of the gully, we would wander up and cross the little stream to find a good place to bury our garbage. After we finished that chore, we would investigate the wonderful caves made of old trees covered in morning glories. It was wonderfully cool and moist in these caves. Sometimes we would walk behind the cabins to the south of our place and come out onto the highway at PCH and Topanga Canyon by the little market with the icehouse. If we were real lucky, Uncle Tom would let us get a penny candy or a soda. The walk home through the soft, dry dust along the Coast Highway was then so sweet.

If we went downstream, we would end up on the beach, a wonderfully endless place of discovery. There were so many stones and shells and creatures to find in the tide pools; we could never bring enough of them back with us. Needless to say, smells in and around the cabin were sometimes less than fresh when the shells we brought back were left inside and forgotten. Some days we would take a picnic lunch down to the sand and spend the afternoon at the beach, and other times we would cross the highway and go to Delong's, a café with a huge counter where they served hamburgers with onions, lettuce, and tomatoes. Cold Cokes were also available in their green bottles. The place had a wonderfully fragrant greasy smell that made your mouth water.

We had some friends who had a cabin at the point behind Delong's Café. They were the Neufelds/Panites who lived near us in in Studio City. They had two boys our age: Johnny and Danny. The parents were concert musicians, and the grandparents had come from Russia. They were Jewish and we were Catholic. During the summer months when we were all spending time at the beach there was a polio epidemic. Parents were encouraged by their family doctors not to allow their children to go to public pools and to make them take naps every day, no matter how young or old they were. Taking naps was something my sister and I did not like doing, but what could we do? We would flop down on the floor in the playroom off the garage with Johnny and Danny and pretend to be napping for the hour or two prescribed. Then it was back to the beach.

Years later in high school there were some really red faces when our conversations turned to the days of the polio epidemic, and Johnny and Danny would pop up with the news that they had taken naps with the Murphy girls. How embarrassed can you get? Even at the reunions fifty years later we remind ourselves of these red-cheeked moments.

We must have lived our summers at the beach cabin for about ten or so years until we built our pool at 12214. The cabin had been purchased by my mother's parents early in the century, and at first it was located on the beach. Much of the Coast Road beach property had originally been owned by the Los Angeles Athletic Club (LAAC), founded in the city's early days by prominent businessmen, including my grandfather Pedro Domingo Larronde, who was Life Member 100. The Club gave its members 99-year leases, and the members would place their cabins on the leased parcels. For some reason, Grandma's cabin was later moved from the beach to a spot on Old Malibu Road where it still sits to this day.

Egg-Shaped Rock

One day I was at the beach with Grandmother Larronde. She was wearing tennis shoes and a long-skirted bathing suit. We put down our towels and beach basket filled with our picnic lunch. I was at the age of pails and shovels, and I started making a sandcastle. I was using a big silver soup spoon and I had a wonderful favorite rock, shaped like an egg, that I had found on the beach on a previous day. The little cove we were in had a high cliff behind it, and we were pretty close to the water's edge; but the waves were not very big, and we seemed to be safe.

Then there was a huge swell and a run of giant waves. It was all we could do to save the towels, the picnic basket, and ourselves. The rest of my toys, including the spoon and egg-shaped rock, were washed away forever. We returned to that cove on many other occasions in search of those lost possessions but never found them. Even to this day as I drive past that little cove in Malibu, I remember that spoon and that rock, and I wonder if anyone ever found them. This cove is right where Topanga Canyon Boulevard makes a "T" into the

Coast Highway.

North of the cove where the cabins used to sit when the Los Angeles Athletic Company owned the property, the beach is now open to the public. Dotted with lifeguard stands, the wide manicured beaches give sunbathers, surfers, and families a place to spend a nice day by the ocean. In the 1970s, LAAC sold the land to the City of Los Angeles for a pretty penny. I knew the woman who worked for the president of LAAC at the time. She told me that when she opened the letter to see the purchase price, she had never seen a check for so much money.

* * *

One day we were on the sand when we heard a siren. I remember my mother talking to her mother about who might be in the ambulance being taken to the hospital in Santa Monica. We finished our day on the beach and walked back up to the cabin, expecting to find Dad and my uncles there with the day's catch for dinner. But that was not to be that day. The ambulance we had heard had been taking Dad to the hospital. It seems that my father and uncles had gone down to Big Rock to do some skin diving with their new underwater weapons, spearguns that looked like the Devil's pitchfork. Dad was a very powerful swimmer. Because he was short, he hadn't been able to play most sports in school, so he had joined the Hollywood Athletic Club and swam with the water polo team. He was a top player and very strong. In later years that proved to be a blessing. With his broken leg and the decades of problems that followed his accident, swimming was the only sport he could enjoy.

On that day he set off with his inner tube with a gunny sack hanging off it. He had his swim fins on and his spear in hand to do some free diving. Wearing his scuba mask, he took his first swim stroke, but he'd forgotten that the speargun was in his hand. Suddenly, the pitchfork was planted firmly in the shin of his leg that had been broken. The rest was rescue and a trip to the hospital.

When we finally learned of the whole thing, Dad had already had an operation to remove the spear. He was coming out of the heavy drugs they had given him and was speaking in a very strange way. His bed was in a ward with maybe three other beds, and the room smelled funny. I was so small that I couldn't see up into the bed where he was, so I climbed under it. Then I could only hear his "drunken" voice from my position under the bed. It was not the best of times. Mother was crying. I was scared. But the next day we were back on the sand as if nothing had happened, and eventually Dad recovered.

Grandma Murphy

At first Grandma Murphy, Dad's mom, lived on South Berendo Street in downtown LA with her daughter, my Aunt Mabel, and Mabel's husband, Carl. They were all very skinny, and smoked and drank all the time. Grandma Murphy was tiny and wiry, so unlike Rubenesque Grandma Larronde. This tiny powerhouse was also a clean freak who loved to use what she called "elbow grease." She cooked pretty well too. I remember that she loved coffee with canned milk and sugar, and she smoked Camels, drank bourbon, and ate chocolate. She had three boys and a girl. Her son Henry was married to Jane, and Carl was married to Alma, and they lived in their own places. My father was her youngest child.

Grandma Murphy's place on South Berendo Street was the upstairs of a duplex. The woman who lived across the street used to stand in the window in the nude so she could catch the sunlight to pluck her eyebrows, apparently completely oblivious to the fact that she could be seen by the whole world. The duplex was rather small compared to Grandma Larronde's big house and yard. I don't remember much about that place except that there always seemed to be arguments when the Murphys got together and drank. My memories of the duplex don't have the same sort of warmth that my memories of Grandma Larronde's house have. Dad's family was thin and cold, while Gram Larronde was fat and warm.

Grandma Murphy, Aunt Mable, and Uncle Carl moved to Bellingham Street in Studio City after Aunt Mable's only son, Bryan, was born. That house was bigger than the duplex but not as big as our house at 12214 or Gram Larronde's at 1844. This is where I really remember the fights at holidays.

Aunt Mabel was my godmother and Uncle John my godfather. At the house in Studio City, her son, Bryan, kept parakeets in his room. There were four-poster beds in that house, and the bathroom had a funny smell. Mabel's husband, Carl, molested my sister Suzanne in that house. He was confronted, but I was not privy to that conversation. Suzanne got major support and attention, and he got the boot—for a while.

Grandma Murphy had lots of old clocks we used to wind. It was a special rite of passage when you were finally allowed to wind the clocks. Her couch had a wooden back and arms that I used to knock my head on. Gram had a TV and loved to watch ball games and prize fights, all kinds of sports, actually. That's what the Murphys did: watch televised games together and argue. They discussed politics and drank and smoked. I was not fond of that house. Carl had a string of DUIs, and Mabel kept taking him back until she finally refused to bail him out. Then he disappeared on the streets of Los

Angeles never to be seen again, and she had to wait seven years to declare him legally dead.

Grandma Murphy became senile at that house and started to talk to me as though I were her sister, and then she went to a rest home in Santa Monica and died at ninety-seven after having six or seven heart attacks on the same day. Dad, her youngest child, had died before she did. Mabel died years later in Spokane after having had both her legs amputated. Her son, Bryan, had gone there to live and work. He is a college professor now and married to Lynn, a former nun and college teacher, and they have four children. They say he has a drinking problem. I couldn't say. But if he does, it would come as no surprise. He still doesn't like the Murphy girls because he says my sisters and I were always held up to him as examples of how to be, and he thinks he can never be as good.

The Best Birthday Present

The best birthday present I ever had was the party my folks gave me and my friends when I was ten, which included a carnival ride at our house. The ponies were live. My parents set up the ride on our front lawn where the whole world could see it. All my friends got to choose the pony they wanted and ride as long as they liked. It was unbelievable. I felt so special. So good. So loved. So wonderful. No one had ever had such a fabulous gift. I will never forget it. I can still feel the sun on me as I rode my pony around our front yard. The world was mine!

Excitement at 12214 Viewcrest Road

We lived in an area of Studio City that was hilly with lots of small canyons. Streets ran up each canyon, with houses built along the sides. Behind our home, the hills were covered with eucalyptus. Lots of streets were dead ends, including the one we lived on, and people often abandoned their unwanted cats on those cul-de-sacs. We always had cats after our Great Dane, Fritzie, was sold to the man with the walnut groves. The other thing we had more than most were fires. Sometimes the fires were caused by smokers tossing butts from their cars; sometimes when power lines sparked and caught the dry grasses on fire. My mother got a reputation as a feeder of stray cats and a firefighter.

Once a fire started in our dining room when a plug arced, sending sparks through a drape which burst into flames. It was a cold, lazy morning, and we were all still warm in bed. When Mother saw the fire from her room, she ran outside, grabbed the hose on the patio, and began spraying the dining room window. Needless to say, the glass prevented the water from reaching the flames. But she seemed unaware of the problem and just kept spraying the window.

I had to dash past the flames to reach the kitchen and pull my youngest sister, Chrisy, to safety. When we were out in the front yard, I found another hose. I dragged it through the front door and into the dining room where I put out the fire. In the meantime, my sister Suzanne had called the fire department while Mother kept watering the window.

Aside from creating lots of smoke damage, the fire was relatively minor. But Mother was never able to explain her actions, and Dad often teased her about it. He was probably away on a business trip at the time. As a traveling salesman, he was often absent from the excitement at 12214.

Dream House

Dad used to tell a story about a contractor who was very successful. He built many fine homes and took great pride in his work. Many people in the construction business wanted to work with him or learn from him. One young man in particular was very eager to have this contractor as his mentor. After a number of years, the young man finally got to work next to the contractor and watch how he did things. The young man also took classes and finally became a contractor himself.

By this time, the older contractor had decided he would take his wife on a trip around the world. It would be the trip of her dreams, the one he had always wanted to give her. The mentor asked the young contractor to build a house for his wife while they were gone. He planned to surprise her on their return. The young man took the plans and the money for the materials from the contractor, and the contractor and his wife set off on their trip around the world.

When the young man reviewed the plans, he immediately realized that this house was going to be full of expensive, extra-special features which he had more than enough money for. Then he began to think. He had a wife who deserved a nice home too, and if he just made a few changes that would never be noticed, he could pocket the unspent monies and build his own wife a house at the same time. So he set to work on finding all the extra-special expensive features you could not see, and he replaced them with cheap substitutes. His mentor would never know. Besides, the young contractor wasn't even being paid to do this job.

The year passed. The contractor and his wife had a wonderful trip, and the house was all ready to be moved into when they returned. The day finally arrived, and the two men met at the lovely new home.

After taking a tour of the house, the master contractor turned to the younger man and said, "You've been so good about this project while I was away, and I wish to thank you for all you've done. Please accept these keys to your new home."

I Want This

In 1950, when I was twelve, the movie *Cheaper by the Dozen* came out. We drove into Hollywood to see it, and no doubt we went to Brown's Restaurant for a hot fudge sundae afterwards. Brown's was where Mom and Dad had their first date. Its high-backed booths made of dark wood with curtains made them perfect for privacy. The seats were red and the wall-paper was flocked with soft fuzzy stuff that was fun to touch.

I was just beginning to think about my future life, and this movie made me realize I wanted a big house and lots of children. It's an image I have kept in my mind all my life: big house, lots of kids. There were cooks, drivers, housekeepers, and gardeners in the movie, as well as in my own life and home; they weren't there all of the time, but often enough for me to think of them as possibly being a part of my future life. It was definitely a preteen's one-dimensional look at life, totally unaware of reality with its stress, problems, and struggles. I was just seeing the lovely home and the beautiful clothes worn by a seemingly stress-free mother running the household with her husband. The children were happy, nurtured, and having a good life. It was inviting, appealing. And I wanted it.

My Stamp Lessons

When I was about ten or twelve, Uncle John gave me and my sister our very own books in which to collect stamps. The idea was that Suzanne and I would learn about history while collecting something tangible from the past and keeping it in a safe place. We were also supposed to learn the value of money. We were expected to use some of our allowance to purchase the stamps, and those stamps we saved were expected to grow in value.

But I was to learn something quite different.

In our neighborhood near the market Mother frequented was a small shop that sold stamps to collectors. It was run by a man who I learned firsthand was a pedophile. Mother would drop us off to spend time stamp collecting while she went grocery shopping. Quite quickly I realized I didn't want this man reaching into my undies while I made my selection.

I let my mother know I didn't want to collect stamps and why. "That man in the stamp store is putting his hands up my panties."

Her response was, "You'll make up any lie to get out of doing what you don't want to do."

So I was expected to go back to the stamp store with my little sister each week. I'm not sure when or why Mother stopped dropping us off at the stamp store, and about thirty years passed before I realized I still had a huge banker's box full of sheets of stamps. Over the years each time I went to the post office to buy postage, I would always get a sheet of the latest issue stamp, take it home, and put it in the box. After all that time, I had quite a collection of stamps for no apparent reason. Then in the course of therapy, I had one of those big "Aha!" moments.

I was still trying to prove to my mother that I really *did* want to have a stamp collection. I also learned that my mother never had my back.

I saved stamps in that box till age forty-five, when I finally got it and let go.

At age forty-nine when I asked my mother about the stamp man, she said, "You'll say anything to get attention."

Busted

It was Thanksgiving. I was about thirteen, the firstborn. In my mind, I was perfect. Suzanne was four years my junior, and I had never quite gotten over her dethroning me. Dad and his brothers were retelling, for the umpteenth time, the story about when my Uncle Henry was shooting his shotgun in the backyard. My dad had gone to rehang the target at a distance he said the gun couldn't possibly reach. As Dad bent over to place the target, Henry fired the gun prematurely, and that's why every time Dad had an X-ray he had to explain why he had buckshot in his balls. As usual, everyone was laughing at the story. That is, except Suzanne. She had a look on her face that told me I was in trouble. Big trouble.

You see, as I said, I never really liked that she had been born and messed up my life. So I had done some pretty awful things to get her in trouble and make her look bad so that she would give me back my throne.

As the laughter subsided, Suzanne got the attention of the grown-ups by saying she had a story to tell. My gut tightened as she began to speak.

"Do you remember?" she said, addressing our parents, "when you thought I'd put Mom's new lipstick all over the bedroom door mirror?"

"Yes," Dad replied.

"Well, I didn't do it. Kathleen did! She put the lipstick only on the lower half of the mirror where she knew I could reach."

My butt slid a bit in my chair.

"And that second tube of lipstick that was ground into the new rug in Mom's dressing room?"

"Yes?" Mom said.

"I didn't do that either. Kathleen did."

"And what about the third tube of lipstick smashed in the carpet at the foot of my bed?" Mother asked.

"Not me. Kathleen."

My butt slid further in my chair. I was almost under the table. All eyes were on me.

"Yeah," Suzanne said. "She did all that. She didn't want me to be able to listen to the radio. And you punished me by taking that privilege away from me."

True, I thought. She was always making noise so I couldn't hear my programs. It had been so much better when she wasn't there. But that was then. This was now—almost ten years later. It was too late for me to be punished, but clearly my cover was blown. I'd been busted, and I needed to come out from under the table.

Free to Be Me

When I was in junior high, my dad really wanted to keep me from being a typical teen. After I was chosen to speak at graduation, he helped me write my speech entitled "Individuality." At its core was his belief that each of us is special and we don't have to do what everyone else does to be accepted. As a result of his influence, I didn't wear makeup or join a social club, even though I was asked to, and my dress code followed rules of modesty, cleanliness, and comfort, not fashion or price. In high school, I was selected by the Rotary to be Miss North Hollywood, and the American Legion sent me to Girls State in Sacramento. Teachers gave me high honors at year's end, and my classmates elected me to Student Council. Dad was very proud.

As I look back on Dad's lessons, I realize I have been able to live my life free to be me without fear. The older I get, the more I appreciate all of his lectures. His favorite question to me was "If everyone cut off their nose, would you?"

Bali Brassiere Company

When I was a teenager, my dad was Vice President of the Bali Brassiere Company of New York. We had been all set to move there when I was in sixth grade and he was first employed as their traveling salesman. But instead, we stayed in Studio City so he could be in charge of the newly created West Coast Department. Up till then, Sam and Sara, the owners of Bali, had catered to the East Coast matron whose figure was not suited to youthful West Coast fashion. Part of Dad's job was to design a more youthful garment for a younger body type.

So he took the sun porch, where he'd spent long stretches of time in traction in a hospital bed, and turned it into a sewing room. A decade before he started at Bali, he had been a cutter at another lingerie manufacturer, Hollywood Maxwell, so he knew how the parts of a bra worked. But he needed a live model. Mother was too matronly, having had three children. My sister Suzanne, four years my junior, was flat chested, and my little sister was just too young. So I got the job, along with my girlfriend Barbara.

This meant that Dad would sew on his industrial machine to produce his idea of a youthful garment, and I would wear his creation at school all day long. I would come home at night and report on how the bra felt on me. Lucky for him I had a very sensitive rib cage and was able to give him the feedback he needed to tweak the cut before sewing yet another version of his idea. The final version, called "The Snowflake," became the bra Janet Leigh wore in *Psycho*.

The Happy Pill

While Dad was working as a designer and vice president at Bali, he did lots of entertaining. I remember caterers swarming all over our home to get things ready for a big event; placing tables around the yard; bringing in extra chairs, table-cloths, dishes, glasses, and silverware; and setting out trays and trays of food for the guests. A bar with bartenders dressed in black made a nice contrast to the caterers in white.

Then came the inspection by Dad. We would all line up to be sure we looked perfect. And then we would get a mini lecture on not talking too much during the party.

My parents' strict attitude here was interesting because my father was an alcoholic and my mother probably had border-line personality disorder and was definitely codependent. Both of them abused me physically as well as emotionally when I was growing up. Also, Mother didn't want me to begin with.

When my father had these parties, which was often, he would start by giving us girls a Miltown, a mild tranquil-izer called "the Happy Pill" in Hollywood, to keep us on our good behavior. Dad definitely didn't want us telling any family secrets at those backyard parties.

What a joke! At the time, people in Hollywood were using this first-ever psychotropic drug for its seemingly miraculous effects as if it were the answer to all their problems. And Dad was always trying to control his family so we wouldn't shame or embarrass him. God forbid we should say the wrong thing. What would people think?

That Hair Cut

It was the day of my high school graduation, and I was getting my hair professionally styled for the big ceremony later that afternoon. I had long hair which I usually wore in a bun, a French roll, or a ponytail. We had a pool so my hair was usually wet. I was not used to beauty parlors or beauticians, and I was relatively clueless as to what the beautician would be doing to my hair that day.

The beautician told me that since I would be wearing a graduation cap, I would need to let my hair down. But first, it needed to be thinned. She made it sound so lovely, and off she started. She washed, thinned, shaped, set, dried, and combed out my long locks. The purpose of the washing and curling was self-evident, but the scissors with the teeth were a mystery to me. There was some teasing done along with some hairspray to hold the hairstyle all in place for the big event.

When I left the salon, my cap was working great on top of my new pageboy haircut. I headed to the school and grad-uated with my class.

When it was time to dress for grad night, I removed the cap to put my hair in a French roll. I realized with horror that I had no hair to speak of for a French roll, a bun, or even a ponytail. My hair was soooo thin that I looked like a drowned rat, like I had just gotten out of the pool. I was so mortified, I cried. I couldn't possibly go to grad night!

Aunt Mabel gave me a shot of sherry, which helped, but I still really didn't want to go to the party. A second shot of sherry put me in the mood, and off I went with my date Steve to the gym, where we were locked in for the night. Fortunately, the lights were low and the music was perfect for dancing, and I soon forgot about my hair. At about 5:00 in the morning, we were all hungry for some real food, so we made our way to the original Bob's Big Boy for breakfast. Then when our tummies were very full, we headed back to my house. We all changed into our swimsuits and dove into the pool, where my hair issue totally disappeared. We all took a long nap on the deck lounge chairs till the sun drove us back into the pool.

My high school friends and I will meet at the Sportsmen's Lodge in Studio City for our Sixtieth High School Reunion in September. If Steve shows up, it will be the first time we have seen each other since graduation night.

My Father's Obsession

My father was obsessed with virginity. It was the highest possession a woman could bring to her marriage. Since he had three daughters, he had plenty of time to preach his sermons on the subject. He had a strange way of going about it, though. He would get a little tipsy, then he would get sentimental, and then he would start telling us about how it was when he was growing up. According to him, he was quite the wild one. He had lived life to the fullest and survived to tell the tales.

Oh, how he loved to tell of his escapades with guns and

dynamite and slingshots and drinking and smoking and then bedding all the women he ever dated. These tales were told with the warning, however, that of course we were never to do any of these things, and in particular, we were not to be one of "those women." Mother, naturally, was not one of "those women." That was one of the reasons Dad had married her.

But the seeds were planted, and in my mind, if not in my sisters', the desire was to grow up and do what grown-ups did, which included drinking, smoking, driving, and being bedded.

To keep us in that state of virginity that my father valued so and wished we would value too, he would insist on meeting our dates. It was not uncommon for him, of an evening, to be cleaning his Browning Over-and-Under shotgun in the living room as my date would arrive and be introduced. When my date and I headed for the front door, Dad would call out after us, "Be sure and keep your legs crossed, Kathleen." If that didn't act as a not-so-subtle deterrent to those poor boys, well ...

One Earring

My father always gave us, his three girls, fabulous pieces of jewelry in our Christmas stockings. The gifts came from a Beverly Hills jeweler. We also got big boxes from Bullocks Wilshire Department Store, filled with magical dresses that made us feel like princesses. I loved this way of celebrating the holiday.

I hadn't thought about this tradition for years, until recently, when I ventured into my jewelry box and saw it: the single earring. And bang, I was back in college and having so much fun on my own. In addition to what I call *fun*, I was also making some typical teenage mistakes. The biggest one was wearing those lovely stocking stuffers on dates. And losing one in the backseat.

The following Christmas I got one earring in my stocking

College and Madrid, Spain

Natalie Wood

It was September 1956, and I was a freshman at Scripps College in Claremont, California, located next to Claremont Men's College (now called Claremont McKenna). As a prank, the boys at CMC had sent their freshman class president on a trip to New York, and that night he was flying back to California.

I drove with some other students from Scripps all the way to LAX to be party to the return of the freshman class president. Unbeknownst to us, Natalie Wood was on the same plane and had attracted quite a crowd of media folk who were milling about on the tarmac at LAX. My friends and I were all gathered at the foot of the stairs to the plane. We looked up to see this sweet young man being kissed by the famous actress. Then I almost had a heart attack because right behind the loving couple coming off the plane was none other than my mother and father who were returning from one of my dad's business trips to New York.

With nowhere to hide, all I could do was own up to what was right before my father's eyes: I was not in class. I was not in school. I was off campus by a country mile and in deep trouble. But I was no longer under my dad's jurisdiction. I was living in a dorm in a college and protected by distance, and I had a loving father who knew I was just having some good fun. I was very glad Mother was not the only one coming off the plane. She was never as forgiving as Dad.

Dad's Advice

Funny how you remember some things forever. My dad was always giving advice: some good, some not so much. But he always gave advice with the intent to make my life easier, better, happier. He believed each successive generation should have more, be happier, and get more education than the previous one.

When I learned to drive and found myself at college without a car (freshmen could not bring their cars to school), Dad told me, "Whenever you borrow someone's car, ALWAYS return it with a full tank." So when I needed to get someplace, I would ask to borrow an upperclassman's car, and by following Dad's advice, I never got turned down.

He was also fond of saying, "Whenever you're with someone and the circumstances warrant it, feed the person you're with. If they're in your home, offer them something to eat. If you're out, treat them to a snack or a meal. And when you call on them, they'll be more inclined to respond."

The Big Picture

In 1957, when I was a sophomore at Scripps, Sputnik first passed over the United States. We were very fortunate that the college was located in an area of Southern California that was still sparsely populated, allowing us to see the night sky more freely than if we had been in a big city. And we were far enough from the coast that the night sky was free of fog and clouds. The college had four dorms that faced large lawns, and a few girls from each dorm had gathered on the green. We lay back on the grass and looked skyward to see what we could see. One of the girls had brought her violin and another her flute. When someone spotted a tiny flashing light moving in an arc from east to west, the girls began to play something appropriate.

Little did I know at the time that twelve years later I would be lying on a green wool carpet in a huge Spanish villa with my second husband, Ahmed, watching TV and hearing Neil Armstrong say, "One small step for man, one giant leap for mankind." Seeing Neil Armstrong and Buzz Aldrin talking from space, walking on the moon, and then planting the American flag was almost unbelievable.

But it wasn't till I turned forty-five and the cell phone was introduced that I would really be personally affected by all the technological wonders. It's not that I don't appreciate all that came before, and I know it is all part of the big picture in technology; it's just that now I can hold my smartphone in my hand and connect with the parts of the world I need to with the touch of a button.

At eighty-one, this is the sweetest thing imaginable. I can't drive or travel much anymore, but I can still attend class plays, soccer games, and concerts via Skype and FaceTime. For me that small step has led to a world I get to share with family and friends. It keeps me connected and alive and feeling part of the big picture.

Caught

When I first went off to college, I found the freedom there unbelievable. From the beginning school and studies became secondary. Dating, driving, drinking, smoking, and ultimately being bedded were my prime focus. I was being a grown-up.

When spring break during my junior year came, I invited a man with whom I was sleeping to dinner at my parents' house. While we were waiting for the meal to be prepared, my father arrived home from work. It didn't take him two minutes to size up the relationship between me and my male companion. Once dinner was over and our dinner guest had departed, I learned just how obsessed my father truly was with virginity, my virginity. It should be noted that he had already moved me from one college to another, from Scripps to The College of the Holy Names, because I was having too much of a fun social life, winning beauty contests right and left, and not getting the best of grades.

I had not followed my father's advice and was now going to pay for my indiscretions. My father was going to do everything in his power to break up this affair. What he did was offer me a trip to Europe on a student tour: three months, seventeen countries. Suzanne had been awarded three months in Belgium with AFS, the American Field Service. But my father didn't feel she should get to go to Europe before I did, so we would both go at the same time—at least that was the rationale he used when telling friends and family of his decision.

I was so torn by this turn of events. At twenty-one, I was totally dependent on my father and mother, and I couldn't imagine not accepting this generous gift. My lover encouraged me to go. "Have a good time," he said. "I'll be here when you get home." I went with extremely mixed emotions.

What this trip turned out to be for me was a mix of exposure to wonderful old-world sights and experiences in a whole new world of freedom, a freedom without rules. I was still just reacting to my father's confusing stories about how wild he had been in his youth and how tame I was supposed to be. Most confusing was this so-called punishment for having broken the virginity rule.

The European Tour

We started in the British Isles, sailed to Scandinavia, took a train, and then travelled across the continent on a tour bus. As I went from country to country with my tour group, I found that my youth and beauty were a great attraction in themselves. I attracted men and boys at every stop we made. Some tried to kiss me right off; others took me out for wine or beer and then tried to kiss me. At first, I was so miserable because of the separation from the man I was having an affair with that no one looked even remotely appealing to me.

As time passed, however, I began to be persuaded by all the attention I was getting that I could enjoy myself. The problem was that enjoyment came with a little too much to drink, and in that condition, I let men I dated get past that first kiss. But never much past it. Something was holding me back. I knew I wasn't the horrible person my father had assumed I was. By the time we got near the end of the tour, I was learning to have a good time and keep my dates at arm's length.

* * *

The day we were scheduled to see the sights of Paris was not that different from the other days of the tour. Much like a swarm of bees, our group made its way about the city, in and out of our tour bus and in and out of shops, mostly sticking together. Once in a while we'd get separated but we would soon regroup.

When we reached the entrance to the Eiffel Tower, we saw a crowd in front of the elevator. People from different countries were waiting to get to the upper platforms where they could view the city from on high. Our group, plus others, squeezed into the elevator. The levels we had access to were midway up. Above that was a level with a radio station and above that lots of antennas. As we slowly rode up in the elevator, we heard much conversation in different languages and people were taking pictures—the usual.

Then the totally unexpected happened: something rather large fell past the window of the elevator. The response was at first silence followed by gasps, then lots of frantic conversation in multiple languages. We all turned automatically to whoever stood next to us. In my case, it was a total stranger who spoke a language I had never heard and couldn't understand.

The elevator slowed to a stop and reversed its course. Someone who spoke English had collected enough information from people who had had a better view of the object as it fell, and she was able to confirm what we'd all pretty much figured out on our own: someone had jumped or fallen off the Eiffel Tower and was probably lying dead where they had landed below. We heard sirens in the distance, getting closer and louder. Needless to say, our ascent was never completed, and our descent was slow and very tense. Tourists couldn't be let out of the elevator until the body was moved into an ambulance and taken away.

When our group finally reconnected with our guide, we were led away from the tower quickly and taken on a nice leisurely walk along the Seine. We were all in need of a glass of wine and soon found a café to accommodate us. Even now, over fifty years later, I can't think of Paris and the Eiffel Tower without seeing that body fall past my view of the city.

A Real Italian Bikini

It was 1959 and I was twenty-one and walking down the street in Rome with two girls on my European student tour. We were being followed by three Italian boys who were practicing their English. My friends and I were looking to buy bathing suits, and the hotel suits were way too pricey. So eventually we let these three eager fellows lead us to an Italian store with wooden tables piled high with clothes, including swimsuits.

After much trying and giggling and staring, we each bought a suit.

I got a blue bikini.

I liked the way it fit.

Then, it was early evening at our next stop on the tour. There were no sandy beaches nearby, just concrete walls with metal ladders leading down from the promenade, which was filled with early evening strollers. I climbed down to the water and waded out into the Mediterranean Sea in my new bikini, attracting a bit of a crowd.

I think they thought I was someone famous.

It was silly—and kind of magical.

When I returned home, my mother threw my bikini away.

Madrid, Spain

By the time we got to Spain, it was the end of summer. We had spent a day or two in most cities. Our time in Madrid and Toledo was to be no different.

It was a lovely late summer day. We were winding down our trip and getting ready to head back to the States. In the elevator of our hotel we came upon a group of men. They were three or four in number, and we were probably five or six.

One of the gentlemen in the elevator spoke English but none of us spoke Spanish. This gentleman turned out to be an attorney who was visiting friends in Madrid. He explained to us that one of their group was a bullfighter, and he introduced us to Jaime Ostos.

The men asked if we would like to go and see the *Plaza de Toros*, the bullfighting ring. Without hesitation we all agreed. After exiting the elevator, we piled into a bunch of little cars that took us to the structure where the bullfights took place. The men took us around the bull ring with the bleachers above it, and then they led us below ground where we saw the corrals for the bulls, the changing areas for the fighters, the surgery rooms for stitching up gored sides, and a room that held a statue of the Blessed Virgin, who awaited the trophies of ears and tails that would be presented in thanks by the winners.

As we came up from the underground area, someone said they were thirsty, and the lawyer asked if we would like to go to his condominium for some lemonade. Again, there was no hesitation. So back into the little cars we all piled and off we went to a huge condo complex on the edge of a beautiful park in the heart of Madrid.

Once we were inside, the lawyer came to me and said, "Would you like to see the rest of the condo?"

"Of course."

Then the bullfighter took my hand and walked me toward the back of the unit. We went through a doorway and approached another door, which he opened to reveal a closet. He forcibly pushed me inside, closing the door behind us.

The next thing I knew I was backed up against the wall with my clothes being pulled down. He finished his business rather quickly, and then turned and left the closet with me still in it. I wasn't quite sure what had just taken place. I was mortified. *What had I done to make this happen? Did anyone else know what he'd done?*

I straightened myself up as best I could and slowly opened the door. The hall was empty. I went back to the kitchen, where everyone was milling about and enjoying the lemonade we had been promised. The others seemed to be none the wiser about what the bullfighter had done to me in that closet.

* * *

The next day the lawyer and the bullfighter came and knocked on my hotel door. The bullfighter did not want to see me; he wanted to see my roommate, who he quickly pulled into the bathroom. I could hear her screaming. She was from New York and wore very tight underwear that she later told me was impossible to take off easily. And she was very streetwise. She basically kicked his ass out of the bathroom before he could accomplish his business. He didn't succeed in raping my roommate.

We ushered the two men out of our hotel room with a "Good riddance!" We finished packing in order to make the planned departure time set by our tour director. I felt dazed, confused, and glad to be headed for the Madrid Airport and our next stop in Lisbon.

My First Pregnancy

After three plus months in Europe, I returned to the States and headed north to Oakland to start my senior year at The College of the Holy Names. Time passed quickly and

I almost didn't notice anything was different, until I started having trouble with my clothing getting kind of snug. I realized I had not had a period in several months, and I was drinking a lot of tomato juice with lemon, so I went to the doctor and donated some urine. The doctor's secretary used her name on the test, and the rabbit died, which meant I was pregnant.

Dad wanted me to get an abortion immediately, and Mom consulted a priest. Father Collins suggested sending me off to a distant location to deliver the child and have it adopted out. Dad did not like the idea, so he consulted our family doctor. Dr. Frick told him he had met someone recently at an international doctors' convention who had perfected abortions in the second and third trimesters. This led us to a decision that sent my mother and me in the dead of winter across the North Pole to Geneva on SAS Airlines.

We flew first class and slept on the plane in sleepers made up like those found on a train. During our layover in Copenhagen, we went to a spa for a bath and a massage. Then, refreshed, on we went to Geneva. It was surreal. I was revisiting so many places I had just seen the previous summer. Now they were all covered with snow.

Once at our hotel, we contacted the doctor and arranged to see him as soon as possible. His waiting room was quite different from those I had seen in California. There were no carpets, no drapes, no décor, just lots of shiny wooden floors, tile walls, and a large expanse of open windows looking out on the icy scenery. We went into his inner office and immediately found ourselves in a huge room. He had a large desk in front of a wide, curved wall of windows. To the right of the entrance was an exam table behind a freestanding privacy screen. Mother took a seat in one of the two chairs in front of the desk while the doctor took me behind the screen to examine me. Then I went to sit next to Mother while the doctor washed his hands at the sink behind the screen. He then took his place in his chair behind the desk.

With that magnificent Swiss Alps scenery for a backdrop, the doctor proceeded to agree that indeed I was pregnant, at least three months, and indeed he had the means to terminate my pregnancy. But he would not.

"Why?" my mother asked. "We were told .... We certainly wouldn't have come all this way if .... Why?"

It seems the good doctor had chosen me to pay for all the sins of all the GIs from World War II who had left pregnant women behind when they returned to America after the war. Those poor women were left with no choices, and I would get to know how that felt. No abortion.

Mother and I were speechless and left the office quickly, barely making it down the dark hall to the cold outside. Back at the hotel, we called Dad, and he was beyond furious. Mother and I took a walk in the snow to clear our heads, and we stopped to have some hot chocolate in a little shop. I thought I saw a man I had had a date with in Paris. We didn't get souvenirs. I had mine tucked neatly inside me.

We left Geneva as quickly as we could and made our way back to California over the pole.

* * *

After Christmas break was over, I called school to let them know I would not be returning for the rest of my senior year. I said I had been diagnosed with TB and would be going to a TB sanitarium in Kingman, Arizona, for the cure. That was my cover story. There was even a nurse friend of our family doctor living in Kingman who would collect all my mail at the sanitarium and forward it to me at my parents' home in Studio

City. I, in turn, would mail my letters to her in a large envelope, so she could mail them from there with the Kingman postmark visible for all to see and believe.

For the next six months I lived in different places, starting with the home of a reclusive older woman in San Clemente whose son was a doctor and a friend of our doctor. My father came to visit me several times a week. Mother didn't make the long trip from the San Fernando Valley. My psychological state came into question after about a month or so, and it was decided I needed a more stable environment. So I moved in with the family doctor, his wife, and children. Dr. Frick lived on the ninth hole of the Wilshire Golf Club. Here I was passed off as a member of the family whose husband was in the service in Europe and stationed where there was no family housing. I was going to live in California till the baby came, and then my husband was due to be discharged and would join us in the States. The lady of the house was also expecting, and she delivered shortly before I did. My mother came to visit infrequently, usually at night, when she would take me to a drive-in movie.

During my pregnancy I went to a beauty parlor (something I rarely did) and picked up a movie magazine. There was a story in it about a bullfighter who was dating Ava Gardner. I recognized his face.

On the day I went into labor, Dad picked me up and took me to Barnes Memorial Hospital in Glendale. I was placed in a small windowless room to live out my labor. Dad got them to find a cup of coffee, an ashtray, and the *LA Times*, a real feat since the hospital was a Seventh Day Adventist facility where smoking and drinking coffee weren't allowed. While I moaned and groaned, he drank his coffee, smoked cigarettes, and read the paper to me.

Finally, someone took me in for a hot shower, and then they put me out with anesthesia. When my child was born, it was taken from me before I woke up. There was already a family waiting to adopt. All of this had been arranged by the doctors and encouraged by the Church. All I had to do was sign the papers.

When I awoke, I was in a room somewhere in the hospital. Across the hall a fellow was playing the harmonica, just like Dad used to do. I didn't know if my baby was a boy or a girl or if it was complete with all its fingers and toes. I didn't know what color its hair and eyes were. I never heard a baby cry. I felt numb.

I did not meet her till she was thirty. That day when I signed the papers, I had declared that I would never look for her, and that was that.

* * *

I know all of this was really hard on my father and may have contributed to his early death a few years later. But I also know he never stopped loving me. As for my mother, she made her first trip to Europe with me, but she couldn't tell a soul about it. The fact that the abortion didn't happen may or may not have pleased her; I don't know. I do know she was glad to be rid of the "problem" through the adoption and certainly never forgave me for what I put her through. I had had a girl, but Mother never told me. She knew my child's birthdate but never in thirty years reminded me of it. But when I finally found my daughter and Mother met her, the first thing my mother said to her was, "I always think of you on the 27th of May. You know, that's just one month before my birthday."

Disney

How I Met Fred

Shortly after I gave birth to my child and returned home from the Kingman cover story, my parents began a campaign to introduce me to eligible young men; marry me off, as it were. The neighbors across the street, the O'Briens, only knew the story about how I'd supposedly gone to Arizona because I had TB, although like most people they no doubt suspected otherwise. They had helped me get into Scripps a few years before. Now they told me they knew a nice family in Hollywood whose son, Fred Kuri, a fine boy, had graduated from USC with a BA in Cinema Studies. His father was the head of the art department at Disney and responsible for the design at Disneyland. Fred had just broken up with his high school sweetheart, and the O'Briens arranged for us to meet.

When the afternoon arrived, I was more than nervous. I was still a bit plump from my pregnancy and not quite past the postpartum bleeding and blues. Fortunately, the doctors had given me some pills to dry up my milk so I wasn't leaking. My hair was very long, and because of the heat, I had it up in a modified French roll. I wore a blue cotton sheath and low heels. Mother, Dad, and my sisters were all in the living room. Through the window, we all watched Fred pull up in his white Ford Fairlane and step out. He was wearing a suit and tie and looked very handsome. His Arab blood—his father was Lebanese—and his youth made him more exotic than any man I'd ever dated.

I greeted Fred at the door and invited him in. Introductions were made and drink orders taken by my mother. All the girls went to the kitchen, leaving the men alone to talk. Mother sent me back out to the living room, and my sisters brought some cheese and crackers. In a while, she came back with the drinks. She was so nervous that she had made Fred's scotch and soda with sherry and given me a shot of scotch in my sherry glass. We all had a good laugh at her expense, but it did break the ice.

Once our drinks were finished, Fred said we needed to leave to be on time for our reservations. He had asked the O'Briens what kind of food I preferred and learned I liked Mexican food, so he took me to El Coyote in Hollywood for dinner. After that, we went to the Egyptian Theater to see *Ben Hur*. We held hands in the movie and afterwards we went to Brown's for a hot fudge sundae.

Though Fred didn't know it, he had duplicated my parents' first date (different movie, same theater). This set the stage for me to believe that he must be the man I was supposed to marry. We made the perfect match: two slightly used and slightly broken kids in need of a partner who might not notice the other's faults.

* * *

My family home of over twenty years in Studio City was up for sale, so by the time Fred had popped the question—after considerable hinting on my part—my parents had all but moved out. Our engagement party for the family was held in a practically empty house. It was early September and I was due back at school in Oakland for my senior year and graduation. Fred was actively working at Paramount and Disney, and my family was moving to Malibu.

I had been advised by the Church not to discuss my past with my fiancé. The woman who delivered my child, who is my friend to this day, said I shouldn't keep secrets from my husband-to-be. I told Fred everything, and he still loved me.

This was more than I could have hoped for.

Over the next nine months, we courted via daily phone calls and letters. To cut down on expenses, Fred figured out a way to make calls from pay phones and charge them to numbers chosen from the phone book. I was too afraid to lose him to say I didn't think that was a good idea. Besides, I needed to hear his voice. On weekends he flew back and forth between Los Angeles and San Francisco to see me at school in Oakland. At the time, PSA ran shuttles for thirteen dollars round-trip. On weekends when Fred would come to the Bay Area, we would venture north to the wine country or south to San Jose to visit Fred's cousins. Sometimes we'd say we were going to visit family and just sneak off alone together. Even though we were sleeping together, we made a practice of attending Mass daily, alone and together, and taking Communion. We considered ourselves already married.

One highlight of the school year was a ceremony known in dorm life as "the passing of the candle," which was strictly for the announcing of anyone's engagement. It happened on Mondays at dinner, and Fred was not going to be able to be there due to his work; he was working at Disney with his father on *The Parent Trap* movie. I talked with Sister Baptista, the dorm mother, and set up the Monday evening when I would announce my engagement to my school friends.

After dinner the candle was passed from table to table around the dining hall. When it finally reached me and I blew it out, everyone screamed. I went up to the mike to let people know my wedding plans. I began by explaining that Fred was not going to be able to join me to share this moment, and that's when the screaming started up again. This was not the usual way the candle passing went, and I had to stop speaking. The girls were now yelling for me to look behind me and when

I did, there was Fred, grinning from ear to ear. He looked so handsome in his suit and tie. I was so surprised I couldn't move or speak. Apparently, the dorm mother and Fred had cooked up this surprise. It was the campus buzz for weeks afterwards.

My Walking Cast

Six weeks before the wedding and five before I was to graduate, Fred came up so we could address and mail our wedding invitations together. After we dropped off several boxes of addressed envelopes at the post office, I took him to the airport in the South Bay and was returning via San Francisco to school in Oakland. The Giants and Dodgers had just played at Candlestick Park, and the fans were flooding onto what was known as the Bloody Bayshore Freeway. A light rain was falling and the pavement was slick. I was driving Fred's VW bug. This was before cars had seat belts.

Before I knew it, I was braking and sliding. My car slammed into the trunk of the car in front of me, a Lincoln with a Continental Kit that held the spare tire. My ankle got twisted between the clutch and the brake, and my head hit the window frame. When my body slammed into the steering wheel, it broke in two. My little car's nose was completely crushed. Things loose in the car had flown all over, some hitting me in the head.

The boy in the pickup truck behind me came over to help. When I stood up to get out, I discovered that my left ankle had swollen up like a balloon. The boy suggested I sit back down. I did so quickly. He offered me a cigarette, and I took it despite the fact that I'd quit smoking. I had blood running down my face from a small cut on my forehead. It took a while, but finally the ambulance and tow truck arrived, along with the police. The police called my college, and the nuns arranged for me to be taken to an Oakland hospital, where my fiancé came after he heard of my accident. Fred and the lawyer for the men in the Lincoln were all waiting for me when I got there.

The school doctor didn't come to see me till the next morning. When he examined me, he took my brace off and manipulated my swollen ankle, which caused me to faint and Fred to turn white and almost throw up. Then the doctor had one X-ray done to prove my ankle was really broken. It was obvious to Fred and me that the school doctor was worse than inept. When my dad finally arrived, he had already set it up for me to be taken by ambulance back to San Francisco to be seen by his orthopedic surgeon.

In the meantime, Fred found his car and talked with the tow truck driver, who had found the small box with our wedding rings, which was one of those flying objects that had hit me in the head. The truck driver told Fred we were very lucky. And Fred agreed, thanking the driver for his honesty, to which the tow truck driver replied, "No. I mean the driver of your car was very lucky. I've towed lots of crashed cars with less damage and the drivers didn't live."

By the time I arrived in a pink ambulance at Heinemann Hospital in San Francisco, Dr. Shermann was waiting for me with pain meds, more X-ray orders, and, ultimately, an operation on my crushed left ankle.

As I was being wheeled into the operating room, there was some lovely music playing. I was really happy from the pain meds and asked the doctor, "Would you like to dance?"

"Sure, if you'll let me shave your leg first," he said.

When I woke up I had a cast up to my hip and I was surrounded by flowers. Dad and Fred were both hovering over me.

Later that morning someone in a surgeon's mask stuck her head in my door. I didn't recognize her and asked who she was.

"I was the nurse during your surgery," she told me. "I just wanted to meet the person who was talking about dancing in the OR!"

* * *

During my recovery, I went through my final exams and graduation from college in a wheelchair and using crutches. When I went to Mass, the bishop of San Francisco had to get up from his throne so that I could kiss his ring—a first for him—since there was no kneeling for me. I got to be the first in line at Mass, which was new for me since my height usually dictated my being at the end with the other tall girls. On the return flight to LA, I got to ride in my wheelchair into the plane in the lift used to transfer the food trays into the galley. Then there were the negotiations with the doctors in LA to get the cast cut down below my knee and a walking post put on so I could walk down the aisle at my wedding.

Despite the wheelchair and crutches, I managed to get through the fittings for my wedding dress, go to luncheons with my bridal party, attend to responses to the invitations, receive the many gifts sent to my parents' house, see Fred on a daily basis for dates, and prepare for my new life as a wife.

Morning Coats and Pinstriped Pants

Six weeks later, in Los Angeles, was my wedding day. I was in a walking cast, but I was able to walk down the aisle of the cathedral, accompanied by my dad with his wooden leg.

The wedding was straight out of Emily Post. The groom, best man, and three groomsmen wore morning coats and pinstriped pants. The maid of honor, junior bridesmaid, and three bridesmaids wore simple, elegant sleeveless sheaths with cummerbunds, dainty satin hats of the same material with a little tulle, and satin shoes dyed to match. They all wore short white gloves. I wore a full-length, long-trained, white satin dress, with cap sleeves and lace at the neck, on the bodice, and down the front. On my head I had a beaded crown with a full tulle veil and my white gloves were long. My bouquet was a cascade of white orchids. Our parents were also formally attired. My mother had white gloves and a pillbox hat dyed to match her dress and shoes. The only jewelry I allowed on the altar were our wedding rings. No one else was allowed to wear any jewelry at the wedding, although they could add to their outfits once the ceremony was over.

The morning event was a full Catholic Mass and wedding ceremony. It took place on Saturday, June 17, 1961, at Blessed Sacrament Church on Sunset Boulevard in Hollywood, the biggest church of its kind in the area and the same place my parents had met in grammar school and later married in 1936. The ceremonies were officiated by three priests: two Roman Catholic and one from the Lebanese Maronite Rite. There was a bell blessed by the Pope and used during that morning's Communion that Fred and I were given as a gift. I still have it. When we turned to leave the altar, I lifted my skirt and exposed my walking cast. At that moment one of Fred's friends yelled out, "I didn't know Fred was marrying a gimp!"

Fred and I left the church in his Uncle Adolph's huge white Cadillac and headed west on Sunset Boulevard for the Beverly Hills Hotel, where several hundred guests would dine on a sumptuous buffet nestled under an ice sculpture of Cupid, complete with crustless watercress sandwiches, shrimp, lobster, and crab, and French Mumm's Champagne. The four-tiered wedding cake, decorated in gold, had a lemon and rum filling. A small string group strolled about the reception, serenading the tables of family and friends. Because of my cast there was no dancing. The toasts were made, and Fred threw the garter and I the bouquet. The table arrangements, like all the flowers, were from George Barnes Flowers in Studio City, and they were taken home by those wishing more than just an extra piece of cake to put under their pillows.

When we changed for our departure, Fred put on a brown suit and tie and I wore a beige silk suit with matching hat, gloves, and one high heel shoe dyed to match. Even with my walking cast, having just the right LOOK was everything. We drove away in a tan Chevrolet Corvair, a wedding gift from my father. Once again, we headed west on Sunset Boulevard for the Bel-Air Hotel for one night in the bridal suite.

I was already pregnant.

Within days of my marriage to Fred, we were spending all the money we had gotten as wedding gifts on an abortion. It hadn't taken him long to realize that he didn't want anyone to think we'd been sleeping together. He feared that if the baby came sooner than nine months, we would be found out. I was already suffering the shame of knowing I was "damaged goods," so with a heavy heart I went along with his wishes. Deep in my gut I knew what we were doing was wrong, but I couldn't risk losing Fred. He knew my secrets, and now we had one together that would guarantee that our marriage would last. We were going to make our marriage look good on the outside no matter the cost on the inside. I knew how to do this. My mother had taught me well.

It was the beginning of the end of a five-year marriage.

Music

The subplot to this fairytale fix of a marriage was that I had come from a family that loved popular music—Crosby, Fitzgerald, Sinatra, and Nat King Cole—and Fred came from a more formal family that loved Beethoven, Mozart, and Chopin. My family was more the beer-and-cocktail crowd, his the wine-and-champagne type. I became the student as my fiancé played all his favorite music and introduced me to a world I had barely heard before. While the music played, he would tell me the stories behind each piece. Our song was from *Swan Lake*.

Sadly, our marriage did not last for lots of reasons, some more obvious than others. But till I die I will always be thankful to this man for exposing me to his passion for classical music. It has been a comfort to me over the years that I grow to appreciate more and more.

Oh, Those Dark Arab Eyes!

My first husband was Lebanese, and he was working at Paramount on a Danny Kaye film when we met. Fred then went over to Disney to do the sets for *The Parent Trap* with his dad. We got to use the bride's bouquet from that set as my flowers for the wedding rehearsal. My father-in-law, Emile Kuri, was Disney's Art Director, and he already had several Oscars on his mantel. He was also in charge of decorating Disneyland. On the side, he did interior decorating for the stars. But what I enjoyed most about his work was that, as a board member of the Academy of Motion Picture Arts and Sciences, he was the art director and set decorator for the annual TV show when the Oscars were awarded.

In the early '60s these shows emanated from the Santa Monica Civic Auditorium. My husband and I got to attend the rehearsals several times. We'd rent a room in Santa Monica and have a mini vacation. Fred would help his father, while I sat in the theater watching whoever was on stage at the moment: Ethel Merman and Nancy Wilson stand out in my mind now. Running into Bob Hope in the halls of the motel was common. While you were sitting in the theater, you never knew who might pass you in the aisle. It was fun.

One day as I sat watching the stage, I had the funny feeling I was being watched. You know how you feel when you sense someone's eyes are on you? Not many seats were occupied, and I felt awkward turning to look around. Just then, my husband came up the aisle from the stage and sat down next to me.

I told him what I was feeling, and he took a look around for me and said, "Oh! That's just Omar Sharif."

It's a Boy

There I was at twenty-four and pregnant with my third child, the first baby I could look forward to keeping.

This time when I got pregnant and returned to my ob-gyn, I was looking forward to my delivery date. One evening during my third trimester, Fred and I went with friends to Dodger Stadium in Chavez Ravine to watch a baseball game. After a lively evening, we returned home and slipped into the welcoming comfort of our king-sized bed and quickly fell fast asleep.

Just about dawn I began to feel cramping in my lower abs and back. When I went to the bathroom I first felt relief, then panic. There was blood everywhere.

My husband carefully helped me out to the car. He lay me on the back seat and then drove like crazy to the hospital. From my supine position, I viewed our drive, our arrival at the hospital, the doctors and nurses who attended me, the clerk who brought papers for me to sign, the arrival of my ob-gyn, and the big blue sheet that was placed in front of me to cut the bright lights in the Operating and Delivery Room.

All the voices in the room were female. My anesthesiologist narrated events for me from the other side of the curtain. When my son arrived and let out his first cry, she declared, "At last! We have a male amongst us."

I was so excited! "Let me see him. Please."

"Yes, of course. But first we have to attend to him and sew you up. "

I drifted in and out of consciousness, and next I saw my family above me: my husband, my dad, my mom, my husband's folks, and my Uncle John. None of them looked like they really wanted to smile. Then the doctor came in and gently explained that little Freddie hadn't made it; and that probably it was a blessing because he had gone too long without a good, oxygen-rich blood supply and, had he lived, he would have been brain damaged.

As I tried to absorb all this information through the fog of the drugs in me, all I could think was, "Can I see my baby? Please!"

Smiles were fading, tears were appearing. I kept asking to see and hold my little boy. I asked if anyone had at least taken a picture of him. No one had. I'm not sure how but I finally slept, and the next thing I knew it was morning.

A nurse came in to wake me for the 6:00 a.m. feeding time for the baby I had lost the day before. When she left the room, she didn't bother to close the door. From down the hall I could hear other babies crying. My breasts hurt and I began to cry too. Dad appeared in the doorway, assessed the situation, and strode back to the nurses' station. I could hear his voice. He was letting the charge nurse know that if this ever happened again, he would report it to the authorities. The way they'd treated me was cruel and unacceptable. When he returned the next morning, he damn well expected his daughter to be resting comfortably. They could anticipate seeing him every day since his office was close by.

And it never did happen again. I didn't get a picture of my son, but they did leave my door closed, and I got to sleep as much as I needed over the next two weeks. Today I know Freddie is right where he should be: in my heart. Dad was the best guy to have on your team.

But I sure would like to have seen my boy. To have held him for a moment.

A Death in the Family

I was married to Fred and living in South El Monte, and I'd gotten my first real job, teaching school. Life was moving quickly for me, but I knew that no matter what happened, my dad would always be there. I was in my early twenties and Dad wasn't even fifty. So when the call came that he'd had a massive heart attack and was in the hospital, I went numb.

Fred and I drove to Los Angeles that Friday after work, and we spent hours with Dad in his room at the Good Samaritan Hospital. He seemed fine to us. As usual, he'd asked me to bring scotch and cigarettes. It was like we were just at home of an evening, talking. Dad was his usual philosophical self and really sentimental about young love, our new relationship, and how much we had to look forward to in our life together. He did talk a little about the "what ifs" should he not make it through this medical episode. But in my mind, he was going to live forever.

So when Sunday rolled around and Dad wanted us to drive to Malibu to visit him at home where the doctor had sent him, I made the decision not to go. I had to be at work on Monday. After only one week in the classroom, I knew I would need all my strength for those kids. Besides, Dad and I would see each other the following weekend.

The visit the next weekend never happened. Very early Monday morning, even before I was out of bed, the phone rang in the dark of our room. It was Mother. Dad had had another massive heart attack in the middle of the night, and there wasn't anything anyone could do. He was dead.

I didn't make it back to my classroom till the following Monday. Fred and I went out to Malibu to be with my mother and sisters, help with arrangements, answer the phone, cook, console one another, and take walks on the beach alone and together. To do all the things that needed to be done.

One of those things was making sure Dad looked okay in the open casket in the funeral parlor in Santa Monica. Mother didn't want to do it, so I was elected. I wasn't sure why this was necessary. Mother was only letting family in for the viewing, and no one in the family wanted to come; the casket was to be closed before the church services.

I remember the funeral director taking me into the visitation room. It was small and dark, except for a light shining down on my father's body in the casket. I was staring down at this man I knew to be my dad and something was wrong. They hadn't combed his hair right, and I told the director this. She gently touched my shoulder and left the room. When she returned with a comb she asked me if I would like to fix my dad's hair and make it right.

"Oh! I can't do that!"

"Sure you can," she said. "It's just like combing your own hair."

At this point I remembered the many times when I was a little girl when Dad would come home from work, make himself a drink, and sit in his favorite chair to relax. I would join him and we would play a game we called "Barber." I would pretend to wash his hair and cut it. Then I would style it just the way he liked it. This memory gave me some courage. So with a little fear and hesitation I put my hands on his head and with the comb began to make his hair right. As the funeral director had said, it was just like combing my own hair, just like playing "Barber" again. By the time I got Dad looking like himself, I had relaxed and felt like any moment he was going to crack a smile, sit up, and say it was all a joke.

Of course, that didn't happen. The funeral took place as planned. Afterwards, we all went to Santa Barbara for a long weekend and came home ready to face living life without Dad.

I couldn't handle it. I had lost both my grams early in life, and Dad had been there for me during those times. When little Freddie had died at birth, Dad had been there for me during that great loss. My husband hadn't been sure how to console me; plus, he was dealing with his own sense of loss. Now I was having to do this alone, and I wasn't doing very well at it.

In fact, I started to see Dad everywhere. Each day I would see at least one car like his and want to follow it. Or I would see a man that looked like him in a store or on the street, and want to go after him. It took a long time before I began to accept his absence. Finally, I learned that even though Dad wasn't there with me in the physical sense, he would always be with me in my heart and mind. I began to see myself dealing with life in some ways just like he had. It was a comfort I'd forgotten.

I had been looking outward to find him when all along he was deep inside me. I could stop looking for him.

November 22, 1963

The afternoon before President John F. Kennedy was shot, one of the boys in my third-grade classroom at New Temple School in South El Monte made an offhand comment about shooting "niggers" for fun back in Texas. He was a disruptive child who often made wild statements to sidetrack the class. As a first-year teacher, I didn't have the experience to handle the situation so that the class could continue as planned. My class included a Chinese girl, the very prejudiced boy from the South, and several Hispanic students.

So for the rest of the day, we held open discussions about such subjects as equality and civil rights; Abraham Lincoln freeing the slaves and how he'd been assassinated; and why people stand up for what they believe in and what price they pay for doing so. Most of the children were very aware of our current president and admired him for his leadership. For a third-grade group, they had a fairly comprehensive discussion. I went home hoping I hadn't let things get too out of hand. I hoped they'd learned something, and I vowed to myself to keep the class on track the next day.

The following day came with a lesson-plan breaker I couldn't have begun to prepare for, let alone imagine. A few minutes after morning recess, the principal came into my room and asked me to turn on the TV. She felt we needed to see the historic event while it was being covered live on TV. This is how we learned that President Kennedy had been shot. The room fell silent. The students watched and listened as the commentator told the horrible story over and over and over. By the time we went to lunch, we knew Kennedy was indeed dead and Johnson would become our new president.

Lunch was very difficult for all of us on campus. Lunches went uneaten. Students didn't play. They just cried and mingled aimlessly on the grounds. By the time recess was over and my class had returned to the room, I realized I was not going to be able to teach the afternoon lesson. I asked the students to come in and put their heads down on their desks for some quiet time. I didn't even turn on the lights.

Pretty soon some of the students began to talk among themselves about the fact that just the day before we had been discussing President Lincoln's assassination and how long ago that had happened. Now we had a similar situation. None of us was quite sure why this terrible event had occurred, but we did know we were all very sad. We would never forget this day.

I don't know what my students learned those two days. What I learned was that no matter what I plan as a teacher, a mother, a wife, I must be ready for the unexpected—and then try and be open to learning the lesson life has in store for me that day. One of those lessons for me is to understand what I can do something about and what I can't, and then let go of what I can't change and focus on what I can.

My Summer Job

When I was teaching in the '60s and married to Fred, I needed a summer job to tide us over during vacation. My father-in-law, Emile, got me a job selling tickets at Disneyland. When I arrived in the mornings I went directly to wardrobe, where I was outfitted in something from the rack that made me fit into the overall Disney theme. I usually got hair bows and a dress with an apron and puffy sleeves, as if I were playing the role of Cinderella or Snow White. I was not allowed to wear makeup or nail polish. That was fine with me since I didn't use them anyway.

Each ticket person was locked in a booth out front at the main entrance to the park. Lines formed early, filled with anxious families eager to get into the park. Most everyone was in good spirits. On one occasion, some frat boys forced a pledge to come to my window and try to convince me he was a prince with no money. As a third-grade teacher I'd heard lots of wild tales and didn't bite. Then there was the older fellow who stepped up and demanded ALL super ride tickets, which I couldn't give him. It seems he worked at Disney, so he took his company ID out of his wallet, shredded it, and threw the pieces at me. All the while he was yelling, "Do you know who I am?" Security had to come to my rescue. I was almost in tears. I never wanted to go back to work. But I did.

I needed the money for rent. We had a two-bedroom apartment with a pool in South El Monte for $99 a month. Minimum wage was about $1.25. Fred and I ate lots of 10-cent Swanson Chicken Pot Pies and popcorn.

Black and White

About twenty-four miles from Studio City where I grew up, is Compton Avenue Elementary School on 104th Street in Watts. A few blocks east of the Harbor Freeway, the school is directly in the flight path for the Los Angeles International Airport.

It is August 1964. I'm going to an interview for my second teaching position. Bright light is reflecting off bare house walls, almost blinding me. Roofs are mostly flat, grass sparse, and trees few and far between. It's warm.

I pull up to the curb and notice several men gathered in front of the housing project across the street. They stop talking and watch this freshly graduated, newly married, and obviously white girl get out of her car and walk into the school.

I am greeted by Juanita, the principal's lovely, loyal, all-knowing secretary. Mr. Thompson may be the principal, but it's immediately obvious Juanita really runs the school.

Impressed that I actually got out of my car, Mr. Thompson hires me on the spot.

Instead of an interview, Juanita leads me down the hall to where my kindergarten room awaits. My brain is packed with songs and games for my new eager little learners, and my closet at home is full of red shoes.

Kindergarteners love bright colors, and my shoes are perfect!

As we walk to the classroom, Juanita lets me know that since there weren't enough children to make up a kindergarten class and since the 5th grade transfer teacher from Vermont never got out of her car, I will be teaching 5th grade.

I try not to panic as Juanita gives me a few words of advice: "Don't smile for at least a month if you want to have any order or control. And if you wish to maintain possession of your purse and school supplies, lock the door every time you leave. Now I'll let you get your room ready."

I stand alone in my new classroom with no lesson plans, the wrong shoes, and the overwhelming realization that they hadn't covered any of this in college.

My first day is crazy with noise and a blur of students who are taller than I am. Several of them belong in junior high but have been held back. I can't help but feel a little like Dorothy in a pair of embarrassingly inappropriate red shoes. This is not the first day I had prepared for or dreamed of.

At the height of all the confusion, Mr. Devereaux, the Special Ed teacher from the class next to mine, appears unexpectedly. He is a professional football player turned teacher with a refrigerator-sized body that fills my doorway.

"If you need any help, Mrs. Kuri, you know where my room is," he tells me. An echo of his powerful voice fills the room, and a hush of respect for this gentle giant settles over my class. He gives them one last look as he turns to leave. My guardian angel has saved the day.

"Thank you, Mr. Devereaux. Thank you so very much."

* * *

It is now the fall of 1964, and although the Civil Rights Movement has begun, there are no laws written or signed to support the kind of equality needed for integration. This means that no matter who you are, where you come from, or how much you make, Watts is the first place you live if you are black and moving to LA. You are not going to be welcomed into white neighborhoods, and your children are not going to be welcomed into white schools. Watts is a required first stop and often a permanent one.

As the weeks pass, I get to know my students better and better. Most of my parent-teacher conferences are held in the students' homes.

Denise is a fashionably quaffed and well-dressed little girl, smart as a whip. Her home is surrounded by a lovely green lawn with landscaped flowers and shrubs. It is by far the nicest house on the street. Draperies left open reveal a beautifully furnished living room.

Ivory lives next door to Denise and is a very tall boy. Polite, shy, and quiet, he struggles with math. His home has a single tree by the curb, probably planted by the city. No curtains or shades. The front window reveals a bare wood floor with a mattress, TV, and a small diapered child eating from a jar of peanut butter.

James is a tight ball of energy. Smart. Witty. Quick. Not inclined to sit and do his lessons. His big black eyes with long lashes glisten. He has a great smile and is a real pain in the neck. I don't know whether to punish him or laugh, and he knows it. Since James has no address on file, I don't think he has a real home.

Denise's mother is an escort.

Ivory's father is a minister.

And James, well, I never met his parents.

* * *

"We're gonna sell more candy bars than you!!"

These words ring through the halls of Compton Avenue Elementary School. The fall fundraiser is upon us and, boy, is it a contest! Each student is sent home with order forms to entice their family and friends into buying the sweet, nutty confections.

Every student longs for their teacher, unrecognizably disguised as a witch, to be the Grand Marshal in the Halloween Parade.

After leading the Halloween parade, and after an unimaginable amount of suspense, the disguised teacher will rip off the mask, revealing the winner to the screaming delight of the entire school. Driven to see me dressed as a witch, my class sells and sells and sells chocolate bars. One day Juanita informs me that my class has won, and it is time for me to go buy yards and yards and yards of black crepe, black tights, long striped socks, a long-sleeved black turtleneck, black gloves, a scarf, a pointy hat, and a mask to disguise my incredible whiteness.

* * *

Well, it's the day of the parade, and Juanita has pulled all the right front office strings to buy me the time I need to make my transformation.

She also successfully helps me stuff and fold fabric to cover every inch of me, so that when I'm dressed, none of the white me shows.

This is it—the witching hour! I confidently march onto the crowded playground. I lead the whole student body past the judges' platform. Success! No one knows it's me. James, my beautiful pain in the neck ball of energy, is being kept in tow by Mr. Thompson, the principal. I take my place beside them as the students start to settle for the big moment.

Then I hear James trying unsuccessfully to contain himself. "Mr. Thompson, Mr. Thompson. We won—my class won!"

I hear Mr. Thompson respond calmly, "James, what would make you think that?"

With his trademark smile, James replies, "Because the witch is pigeon-toed—and so is Mrs. Kuri."

Barely able to contain my laughter, I unmask myself. All my students go wild. Screaming and backslapping follows as they rush in around me. James bellows that he knew all along that the witch was me. I am so proud. And pigeon-toed, apparently.

As the excitement of the victory winds down, Denise takes my hand, and we walk around the playground, enjoying all the day has brought.

A little girl from another class walks up to us and asks Denise, "Is this your mom?"

I can barely breathe.

The world stops for just a moment.

It is so profoundly beautiful.

This is what it looks like to be colorblind.

This is what it feels like.

I stand motionless and humbled, not sure which of us is the teacher.

Me, the Nun

When people first met me when I was fresh out of college and teaching in Watts, they all thought I was a nun. I had been to several years of Catholic school and dressed rather conservatively compared to others on the teaching staff. I carried a briefcase and wore my waist-length hair up in a bun. In those days, teachers had to dress for work: a girdle, stockings attached to the girdle, heels, blouse, jacket, and jewelry. Panty hose hadn't been invented, and women did not wear slacks.

Once I moved on from that teaching job, I found myself

in downtown Oakland feeding street people every morning in a church located behind the City Jail. And again, those standing in line for their meal were always calling me "Sister."

One gentleman, whose name I don't remember, wore a cast on his left arm. When I first met him, he came up to me and said, "Sister, if you are ever in trouble or you need help, call me." With that, he pulled a shiv out of his cast.

I realize now that I was never inclined to correct these people because the title they were giving me was a form of protection in what otherwise were not the safest places for a woman to be.

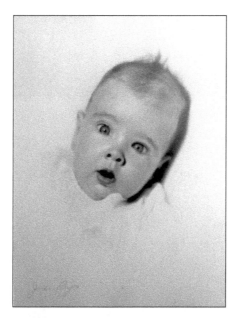

"Hello, World." June 10, 1938.

With Grandmother Murphy, circa 1939.

With Fritzie, circa 1940.

12214 Viewcrest Road, Studio City, CA.

"We three." With Dad and Mother, circa 1940.

Dad recovering at home post auto accident, 1940.

Grandmother Larronde.

Grandma Larronde's house
1844 North Kingsley Drive, Hollywood, CA.

The Larronde House on Bunker Hill. Los Angeles, circa 1900.

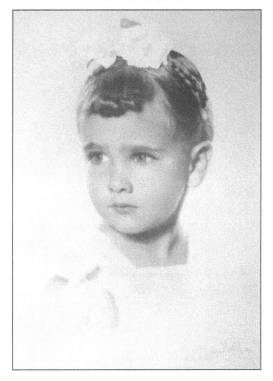

"Excuse me. You're suggesting what?" circa 1942.

WW II, with Uncle John and Suzanne, circa 1943.

With Suzanne and Uncle Jippy, WW II pilot,
twice lost in the Pacific, circa 1943.

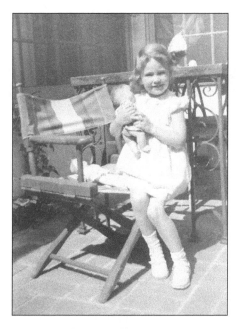

My Ruthie Doll, circa 1943.

Harriet Judy, circa 1951.

The Murphy girls, circa 1952.

My first catch, circa 1952.

By the pool at 12214, circa 1954.

Summer of 1956.

Scripps "Miss Claremont Men's College," circa 1957.

St. Mark's Square, Venice,
European Student Tour, summer 1959.

Dinner in Paris, European Student Tour, 1959.

In the cockpit on the flight from Paris to Madrid, 1959.

Engagement party with Fred Kuri, 1961.

With Dad, 1961.

Wedding day, June 17, 1961.

Cuttting the cake. Beverly Hills Hotel, 1961.

"I didn't know Fred was marrying a gimp!" 1961

Dad's funeral, with Suzanne, September 1962.

Ahmed El-Senoussi's Palisades home
(and I did get to live there after all!).

The pool at Amber Lane in Ojai, circa early 1970.

Playing backgammon with Ahmed on Amber Lane,
circa 1970s.

Sunkist grower's break on Amber Lane, circa 1970s.

Painting the servants' quarters bathroom
before serving dinner for 12 on Amber Lane.

Visiting the Sphynx with Ahmed and his nephew,
the minister of culture. Giza, Egypt, 1972.

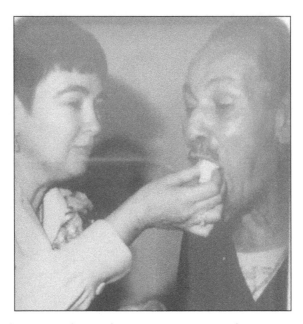

Wedding in Ahmed's room in St. John's Hospital
in Santa Monica, December 18, 1978.

Marrying Marvin Hellwitz in Uncle Jippy's house.
22000 PCH, March 12, 1983.

My new family—
Suzanne, Kris, Marvin, Bryan, and Debbie.

With Debbie, my stepdaughter, circa 1988.

Garage sale with Marvin and the kids in Ojai, 1989.

The four generations: Mom, me, my granddaughter Alcamy,
and my daughter Mary Jane, 1994.

With my beautiful daughter, Mary Jane, circa 1996.

Mary Jane, Alcamy, and Fallon.

Alcamy.

80th birthday party, with Mary Jane, Alcamy,
and Alcamy's husband, Austin. June 9, 2018.

At 702 Canada Street, circa 1990s.

The Bird Lady.

With Mojo, Debbie Murphy's cat.

Kim Maxwell's The Townies, Inc.,
10-Week Workshop in the safest room in Ojai.

Thanks, Kim, for teaching me how to write.

Egyptian Nights

How I Met Ahmed

Shortly after Fred and I were married, Kennedy called up the National Guard for the Berlin Wall crisis, which was actually a cover story for sending American soldiers to Vietnam. As a member of the National Guard, Fred had to quit his job at Disney so that he could work on military planes at Van Nuys Airport. He kept his bags packed in case he was sent to Vietnam. During this period, we lost our newborn son on May 1st, 1962, I got a job teaching in South El Monte, and my dad died in September of that year.

When Fred got out of the service, he decided to go back to school. LSD was becoming popular at that time with prominent academics, and Fred took a turn or two with it. He changed considerably. When I inherited some money, he wanted to use it to buy a boat to travel around the world. It took gall for him to ask for the money, especially since we had been concentrating on buying a house, and there was a lot we could do with the money. I could have bought a parcel of land overlooking the ocean that we could build on later. But the LSD had changed him so. He wasn't reasonable, and he was focused on going around the world, and I wasn't.

I turned for help to our family doctor, who sent us to a psychiatrist from Egypt in an effort to help us deal with our rapidly changing lives. It didn't take the doctor long to realize that our problems were too large for him to handle, so he sent us to *his* therapist.

As we approached the address we had been given, I realized that I was finally going to be able to go inside the house on Sunset Boulevard in Pacific Palisades that years before I'd vowed I would live in one day. When I was a child, every summer my family traveled back and forth from Studio City to Topanga

Canyon where Grandma Larronde had her cabin at the beach. That trip took us along Sunset Boulevard in Pacific Palisades. When we got to the Riviera section, the fanciest section on Sunset Boulevard, my sister and I would call out the house that we wanted to live in when we grew up. She chose a ranch style, one-story house and I a regency style, two-story. Sure enough, I was going to get into my house at long last.

Fred and I had been having a huge fight on the drive over about God knows what. After we parked, we walked around the corner to try and resolve our problem before we went into the doctor's office. That didn't work. So we walked up the steps and rang the bell. The door was opened by a man wearing a loose-fitting white cotton shirt, shorts, and no shoes due to a broken toe. He was smoking a cigarette and had a scotch and soda in one hand as he welcomed us into his home. This was how I met Ahmed El-Senoussi.

He led us directly into his office where we took a seat facing him and began our therapy. The room was lined with bookshelves full of books and papers. The windows on either side and behind Ahmed showed a lovely garden full of flowers, trees, and green grass.

* * *

After several months of going to marriage counseling sessions at Ahmed's home in the Pacific Palisades, Fred and I started going up to Ojai where Ahmed had a second home. Ahmed would take couples up to Ojai on a Friday and they would come back on Sunday. This gave Ahmed the chance to watch the dynamics of each couple as they swam, cooked dinner, and interacted with each other, providing him with a more accurate picture of what was and wasn't working in their marriage. Fred and I were one of many couples that spent weekends at Ahmed's. Although Ahmed went to Ojai frequently, his wife, Ronnie, very rarely came up there, maybe twice in five years.

Then Fred stopped going to the counseling sessions in Ojai. He was done with marriage therapy. Although he was moving away from LSD, he and I were not growing any closer. As our lives started going in different directions, we gradually started to separate. Fred was still trying to persuade me to use my inheritance to buy a boat and travel around the world. When I said no again, he left me. About the time Fred left me, Ronnie left Ahmed. While this was happening, Ahmed and I had become connected, and we began to fall in love.

Ahmed's Youth

When I was married to Ahmed, his sons and I tried to get him to make a tape recording of all of his stories about his youth. Needless to say, that did not happen. So I will see what I can remember.

Ahmed was born into a wealthy, powerful, and politically well-connected Libyan family living in Egypt. He had two uncles. One uncle was the King of Libya, who asked Ahmed to accept his throne, which he declined. The king then gave the throne to his son, Ahmed's cousin, who ultimately abdicated the throne to Qaddafi. Ahmed's other uncle was a medicine man who traveled through the deserts of Palestine, Jordan, and Lebanon, visiting Bedouin camps along the way.

Ahmed was trained by this uncle to care for illnesses ranging from infertility to conversion disorder, an illness caused by stress that would often manifest in paralysis. He traveled on horseback with a dog and a snake, both of whom were named Masaoud, one of the ninety-nine names of God. His horse loved the smell of smoke from cigarettes and would take an occasional sip of scotch. The snake, a very large boa constrictor, would create a circle around its master's body during the night to keep him safe from scorpions and other snakes while he slept. As needed during the treatment sessions, the snake would also deliver messages that Ahmed had previously placed in hollowed-out eggshells.

When Ahmed entered a camp, he would be told about the various people with illnesses who needed attention. Within a very short period of time, and before he began to treat them, he would have to figure out if he could cure this person of their illness. This was especially important because the Amir, the leader of the camp, had the power of life or death over everyone in the camp. And if Ahmed's treatment did not work, the Amir could put him to death. Since Ahmed lived to tell the tale, I would say he most likely was quite successful.

During this period in his life, Ahmed learned to do with and without. He only carried what he needed: nothing more, nothing less. At the same time, he was also training to be a religious leader in his Sufi sect. His training required that he spend prescribed periods of time in isolation, fasting and meditating. He had to do this for seven days three times, fourteen days three times, twenty-eight days three times, and thirty days three times. During these sessions he had to sleep in a cave with a circle drawn in white chalk around him.

Then Ahmed went to England to study at the Tavistock Clinic, which had been founded by Anna Freud. From there, he went to Chicago and then on to Los Angeles where he lived the rest of his life, with homes in the Pacific Palisades and Ojai. He studied at UCLA, Claremont Graduate School, and the United

States International University (USIU) in San Diego, where he ultimately received his Ph.D. in psychology.

Egyptian Watercress

In 1972, when I traveled to Egypt with Ahmed for the first time, I learned many things that were new to me. Several of my husband's friends had also studied in the United States and received their graduate degrees there, but unlike my husband, they had returned to their homeland. In Egypt they had gone into government work or become university professors and ultimately department heads. One gentleman in particular was the head of the Department of Agriculture at the University of Alexandria. As part of his job he communicated with his colleagues in departments of agriculture at universities around the world. Not only did these scientists talk with each other, they also exchanged plants and seeds. California schools were the most popular ones to exchange seeds with. In Egypt they especially liked California tomatoes. As far as I knew at the time, my source being the media, people in America didn't communicate with people in the Middle East unless they were family. Little did I know how wrong I was until I made this first trip to Ahmed's home country.

On a more personal level, while on this trip, I was introduced to lots of good food, some new to me. One vegetable in particular was my husband's favorite, which he called Egyptian watercress. In Arabic it goes by the name *gar gear*. It's a spicy, delicate leaf we would eat by itself or mixed in a salad. We ate lots of it, and Egyptian watercress soon became my favorite vegetable too. Our friend at the University in Alexandria gave us a large pack of seeds as a departure gift.

For years after that, we grew Egyptian watercress in our garden and shared it with our family and friends. As I enjoyed my arugula salad yesterday, I was pleasantly reminded of my first trip to Egypt.

Memories Without Photos

We traveled to Egypt once more before Ahmed's death in 1979. Since that trip, whenever August 8th rolls around and the media reminds us that on that day in 1974 Richard Nixon resigned from the presidency, I find myself reliving that day.

Ahmed and I had spent the day on a fishing boat in the channel off Ventura, California, and we had caught lots of rock cod and halibut. One of our neighbors had joined us, and we made friends on board with a couple of men who worked in construction. It had been very foggy early in the day, but when the fog lifted we had a magnificent view of the rock arch on one of the Channel Islands. I can still feel the layers of the old warm clothes I was wearing that day and feel the warmth of the coffee cup in my hands.

With our catch tucked safely in the car trunk, we got back in our warm car and headed home to fry what we had caught in a batter seasoned with Egyptian herbs and spices for the friends and neighbors who would be joining us for dinner. When we turned on the radio, the first thing we heard was that Nixon had resigned, which was not a totally unexpected outcome following the months of Watergate news.

Ahmed and I began to reminisce about our connection to the now ex-president. In 1973, we made a trip to Egypt where we were entertained by a really famous belly dancer on the rooftop of the Hotel Semiramis on the Nile. The following year, Nixon and Kissinger were entertained by the same dancer. We, however, didn't get our picture with her on the cover of *LIFE* magazine like they had.

* * *

When Ahmed and I traveled to Egypt, we were met at the Cairo airport by his nephew, the Minister of Culture, or his dear friend, a lawyer and the first female member of the Egyptian Parliament. We always stayed at The Shepheard Hotel, where we were visited by family and members of the late Nasser's cabinet. These distinguished men had spent time as political prisoners and they called each other by their old cell block numbers. We often dined with them and their wives in rooftop restaurants where cats roamed among the diners, and we were entertained by that very popular belly dancer. Ahmed had helped Nasser overthrow King Farouk in 1952, and he had private meetings with Sadat on each trip to Egypt. He often referred to himself as a counselor to kings. Many were the nights when after dinner we would walk back to our hotel along the Nile without a care. The streets of Cairo at midnight then were quiet, peaceful, and safe.

On our last trip to Egypt together, my husband was interviewed and our photo was taken for the local paper. But most of the pictures of my visits to Egypt are in my mind and my memories.

* * *

An odd occurrence happened on one trip to Egypt. Back in 1962, when I was pregnant for the second time and had reluctantly agreed to the abortion Fred felt was necessary, a doctor who knew Billy (a medical student friend married to an airline hostess), gave me a treatment called "seaweed in the uterus," designed to make the pregnancy fail. This doctor was apparently kept busy serving the stewardesses of the airline industry. When he had arrived at my door carrying a brown shopping bag, I noticed that he wore a gold pinky ring with a distinctive mottled blue stone.

Years later, Ahmed and I were on board a plane heading for Egypt. There was a medical emergency in first class where I was seated with Ahmed and a friend. The hostess brought an economy class passenger up to first class to deal with the problem. I thought the man looked familiar. When I saw his hand reach out, I knew why immediately. He was wearing the gold ring with the blue stone from a time gone by.

Ahmed Loved to Dance

Oh, how Ahmed loved to dance! Especially to Latin music. How strong his arms were! What fun it was!

Along with dancing in our living room, he told stories of having danced in the nightspots in Cairo and Alexandria, with King Faruk at ringside.

The lovely night air off the Nile.

The sweet smell of flowers from the carts of the street vendors.

The magic of it all in the words he used to tell of his memories.

And then it was the two of us dancing in those romantic locations for real, and it was more magical than I had imagined it would be.

I'm so lucky now to have those firsthand memories of

my own. They make for very sweet dreams now that I am older than he was when we danced in Egypt.

You were right, Ahmed: God does provide.

My Favorite Home

Of all the homes I've lived in, one by far is my favorite: the villa on Amber Lane where I lived when I first came to Ojai in the mid-'60s with Ahmed. The Spanish Hacienda sits on seven acres on top of a hill in the Country Club Estates across from the Ojai Valley Inn. It was built in the 1930s by Henry Ford of the Libbey Owen Ford Glass Company, who had hired the young architect Paul Williams to go to Spain and copy the plans for a villa in Andalusia that Ford especially liked. Later, the architect Williams would go on to design the Beverly Hills Hotel, LAX, and dozens of other homes in the Los Angeles area, but the Amber Lane house was one of his first projects.

When the man in Spain who owned the original villa came to Ojai as Ford's guest, he was amazed to see his home duplicated so completely. Every detail was there: the tile roof, the fountains in the courtyard, and the extra grand living room that opened onto a courtyard on one side and a pool on the other. The library with wood paneling and a fireplace was especially cozy. In addition to the master suite, there were four family bedrooms with attached bathrooms on the ground level. Upstairs were two guest suites with a fireplace in one and baths in each. Each room had its own view of the Topa Topas, the magnificent range of mountains that surrounds the Ojai Valley. The servants' living quarters were off the large kitchen, which was connected to the dining room by a full pantry. The villa had a three-car garage, and storage there was endless. The grounds were lovely and included a tennis court and the pool. According to a man who worked as a young laborer when the house was first built, the massive blocks for the Amber Lane Villa were made in the driveway.

When my husband bought this estate, it had a family orchard and several acres of mandarins. Ahmed was a Sunkist grower and he sold mandarins to the Ojai Valley Inn for use in the fruit baskets they gave to their guests. The Amber Lane house was at once large enough for the many groups we entertained and cozy enough when we were alone there. My husband bought it in the '60s for $60,000 and sold it in the '70s for $250,000. It was recently for sale for eight million. I had a grand time in that home and still miss it. Thank goodness for the memories.

An Evening on the Hill

The house on Amber Lane was a great place to live. Ahmed loved to entertain when we came up from LA to spend the weekend in Ojai. He especially liked putting people together who might not otherwise find themselves in the same social setting. So of an evening you might find the Chief of Police, a doctor, and maybe a lawyer sitting side-by-side at the dinner table with a teacher, a retired grocer, and a bank teller. Plus, Ahmed might throw in a couple of his patients, some neighbors, and even a few folks we ran into in the checkout line at Bayless Market while shopping for dinner that day. Several local radio newscasters and a musician or two might also join us. That was a pretty standard dinner for us.

Before dinner, many regulars would join us in the kitchen to watch my husband cook various foods from his homeland of Egypt. Depending on the weather, we would either take a swim in the pool or gather around the fireplace after dinner. There was always a poker game in the making. As I said, the house on Amber Lane was a great place to live and party.

I especially remember one warm evening in summer. It was after dinner, and everyone was full and relaxed. The dishes were all washed and put away. There were no leftovers. As the light faded, a few folks sat chatting by the pool. One lady with white hair who lived at the far end of town began to talk about how her day had gone. Seems she was really tired all day because her neighbor's peacocks had been dancing all night on her corrugated metal roof. The son of the police chief, who was also the head of animal control, said he would be happy to come speak to her neighbors. Then someone asked why the lady thought the birds were dancing on her roof.

"Well, it may be the peyote I planted recently," she said. "I think they were eating it." As the woman realized what she'd just said to the police chief, she covered her face with her hands and quickly added, "And they ate it all up!"

There was a long pause. We were all looking at the police chief. The lady with her white hair slowly slid lower in her chair.

When the chief finally spoke he said, "And what is your address?"

The woman's reply was quick but quiet.

"Oh, you're way out of my jurisdiction," the sheriff said. "I'll let my son handle it for you."

All at once everyone let out a chorus of sighs. Then came the deep breaths. The subject changed and the evening proceeded nicely for all.

"Poker, anyone?" my husband asked.

Tractor Meets 18-Wheeler on Ojai Avenue

Fifty years ago, Ojai Avenue was so free of traffic that I could easily drive my little Montgomery Ward Squire Tractor down the road to the gas station to have the mechanic show me how to change the oil. At the time, Ahmed and I were living in the Amber Lane Villa, and one of our neighbors was Mr. Goforth, who owned an 18-wheeler cab for his business.

One lovely spring morning I was dressed in my usual overalls, boots, and straw hat. As I drove down the Avenue minding my own business, I had a strange feeling that some-thing wasn't quite right. When I turned around to look, I was almost blown off my seat by a friendly toot from a gigantic truck grill with huge windows that were reflecting the sunlight and blinding me. The driver wasn't going very fast, but the size of that giant machine overwhelmed me. As we passed through the shade of a very large tree, the glare on the windows faded, and I could see my neighbor, Mr. Goforth, who was laughing hysterically. I, on the other hand, was just glad I had not soiled my overalls. To this day I can still feel that 18-wheeler cab behind me.

For the next twenty years I continued working in a man's world and was constantly the object of good-natured ribbing. I have always known more truck drivers and backhoe operators than ladies who lunch.

I have pruned over seven acres of mandarin oranges. More than once I supervised parts of the construction of the new home Ahmed and I were having built on Country Club Drive, including the installation of the cantilevered swimming pool. I have fixed leaky roofs and painted swimming pools and overseen remodeling projects.

Little by little over the years the men I deal with have

stopped asking me, "Lady, are you sure you know what you're talking about?"

Willamina

I often wonder what the priest who baptized me at birth would have said if he knew the name Dad had already put in cement in our backyard—William George Murphy III—in the expectation that I would be a boy. After my parents realized I was a girl, they momentarily considered calling me "Willamina," and then settled on Kathleen. Dad was a traveling salesman, and he later learned for himself it was a good thing I hadn't been given the name Willamina for a handle.

There was a lady who owned a lingerie boutique in Oregon whose name was Willamina. She was very Rubenesque and rather crude, as my father would say. So when he met her on his travels, he thanked God he didn't have any regrets about naming me.

Decades later, I heaved my own sigh of relief when Ahmed and I were living in our custom-designed home on Country Club Drive and I met a new neighbor. Her husband was the night accountant at the Ojai Valley Inn, and they lived in one of the houses the Inn had purchased on Country Club for its employees. She was invited over to our house once. When she drove up our driveway she was quite drunk and behaved crudely. She was scantily dressed and beyond Rubenesque. I came to find out she was the same Willamina from Oregon that Dad had known. Thanks again, God.

Summer Wind

Were Mother, Suzie, and Chris all there that night at Nelson Riddle's recording session when Sinatra sang "Summer Wind"? If memory serves me, they were. Nelson Riddle lived on Old Malibu Road, as did Mother and my sisters. My youngest sister went to school with Nelson's son Chris, and Mother was friendly with Nelson's wife. They went to a lot of his recording sessions.

And where was I? In Ojai with Ahmed, "that Arab," who was older than Mother, which didn't please her at all, so she spent a lot of energy ignoring me or telling people that I was dead. As much as I love Sinatra, I guess I'll never be able to separate him from the reality of my life and how my mother treated me during the '60s and '70s. It is kind of sad, too, because I would really enjoy that music if it weren't for the attached memories.

Mother will be gone now ten years this week, and I don't play much music from my earlier years. I don't need the subtext of pain it creates. I would rather listen to birds sing and wind blow through the chimes in my back yard.

Only Sixteen Years

During the almost two decades we were together, my second husband was in the hospital a lot. When Ahmed was in St. John's in Santa Monica, I visited him daily. Visiting hours were very short and strictly monitored, but he wanted me there every minute. At the time, there were no colorful nurses' uniforms; white was the only color they wore. So every time I passed the nurses' station in my street clothes, I was busted.

Ahmed would get upset when I was denied entry to his room, and his blood pressure would go up. No one was happy. One night while I was drifting off to sleep, the solution came to me. The next day I went to a uniform shop near the hospital and bought three white nurses' outfits and a pair of white shoes. Problem solved.

* * *

Ahmed was thirty years my senior and had smoked since he was five. In those days you could smoke in the hospital. One night while he was at St. John's, he pulled his tray table up to his bed and placed a pillow on the cold metal bar near the floor so he could prop his feet there while he smoked. His lighter, cigarette pack, and ashtray were on the tray table. When he finished his cigarette, he lay back down and fell asleep.

At some point during the night, a nurse checking beds came into his room, saw the pillow, and put it on a chair. When my husband woke and sat up in bed, he put his feet down on the metal bar, but there was no pillow there. His feet slipped, the whole tray table slid out from under him, and he landed on his head on the hard terrazzo floor. His fall created an aneurysm in his forehead that would later require removal.

Meanwhile, I was a few miles away in our home in the Pacific Palisades, sound asleep, with Cleo the cat and Major the dog. At the moment of impact, all three of us shot up in bed. I turned on the bedside lamp and looked at the clock: 3:00 a.m. I listened. No sounds. No one was trying to get in. So what could it be?

I grabbed the phone and dialed the nurses' station. The person who answered said all was well in my husband's room. I hung up and tried to go back to sleep.

Shortly afterwards the phone rang. It was Ahmed who told me what had happened. He had a knot on his forehead, but otherwise he was fine. He said the nurse had asked how I had known to call.

He told her, "My wife is very sensitive and we are very close."

When it was time to remove the tiny aneurysm on Ahmed's forehead, I asked the doctor if I could watch.

"No problem," he said. "It's fascinating."

He was a plastic surgeon and watching him was like watching an artist.

When he was finished, I said to him, "I'd really like to be able to do that someday."

He shook my hand and said, "Okay. I'll see you in fifteen years after you graduate."

Reflection

My reflection:
I look for it in a pool: nymph.
I look for it in a mirror: vanity.
I look for it in your eyes: I live.

* * *

I had such a strong reflection in Ahmed's eyes that I never knew how fortunate I was. Oh, I knew I was happy and fulfilled, but now I look for that reflection and don't find it. It's that knowledge that someone very special knows and cares, and that he sees his love reflected back when he looks at you.

If I search forever, I will never find the same reflection. Not unless it's true that our karmas are locked forever, and then we will meet again as it was said we met before.

Real love is a hard act to follow.

My Secret Service Guardian Angel

Soon after my second husband died in 1979, I began walking on a daily basis. For several years, I had been sitting for endless hours in hospital rooms, and I was overweight. I felt lost. When a beloved husband is dying, a couple of things happen. For starters, you want to go with him, but you also want to live and carry on, and you don't want to subject yourself to what you've just seen him go through. When Ahmed died I wasn't eighty and waiting for him to die. I was forty-two. I really needed to get serious about my own health.

When I started walking, I realized I had something to do in this life; I was here for some reason. Although I may not have been aware of it, I'm sure deep inside I had a desire to find my child who had been adopted out at birth. At the time I was living at 13681 Sunset Boulevard in the Pacific Palisades. The hills behind me provided a very good place to walk. There was a gentle incline at first for warming up. Then as the grade steepened, the road switched back and forth to accommodate both the homes and the street in front of them. The homes I'd pass were often seen in TV commercials or occupied by Hollywood celebs such as George Carlin and Sylvester Stallone, who I would see in his driveway shadow boxing. The higher I got, the harder it got. It was a perfect workout.

But this particular walk also afforded me an interesting reentry education into America. My previous life with my late husband had been immersed in the Middle East and his business as a psychologist, which he conducted in his two homes.

Now I was alone in America again. I was still living in his home with the working gals we had been renting rooms to for some time. One of the women bought me a red jogging suit so I could be found easily if I got lost. Her idea of a joke.

Actually, the suit made it easier for the Secret Service to see me coming. You see, on the hill above my house lived many of those high-profile celebrity types I mentioned, not the least of whom was Ronald Reagan, who had just announced his candidacy for president. My walk, therefore, became an exercise in slipping through the Secret Service lines. Once I passed Sylvester Stallone out for his Rocky walk, and that was the first time I encountered the checkpoint. The first time I was stopped, they wanted my ID. Who carries that out on their exercise walk in their own neighborhood? Not me. But when I gave them my name and address, they found me on their list and I was allowed to pass. No problem. The experience was a bit spooky, but I kept taking my daily walks.

By the time I reached the road leading to the one above the Reagans' house, I would be ready for a drink, and there was a special spot the homeowners had set up for us walkers. These kind folks who lived halfway up the mountain had built a rock watering station, complete with a bowl at the base that could be refilled as needed for your dog and a regular drinking fountain up high for human use. I was always most grateful for those thoughtful folks. Another two switchbacks up and I would hear the silly "ooga-ooga" sound of a horn emanating from an unmarked Secret Service car. As the days and weeks passed, the agent inside and I became friends. This was before cell phones, so there was a telephone line running up the hill from Reagan's house to a phone on the front seat of the Secret Service car. In case of an emergency, the agent could be contacted ASAP.

He and I had some interesting talks. He was also assigned to LAX and was privy to things I had never heard of, including the world-wide sex trade that kidnaps women and ships them all over the place. They get these ladies hooked on drugs, dress them very well, and make them available to men traveling around the country as well as the world. The agent felt that I would make a perfect target for these people and recommended I acquaint myself with mace and take Judo lessons for self-protection.

The last leg of my walk took me to the entrance of an enormous estate owned by a big cosmetic tycoon that was visible from the San Diego and Santa Monica freeways. At the time I was working at St. John's Hospital in Santa Monica where my husband had died only a short time before. I got the mace, but married a cop before I got around to taking Judo lessons. Today my former boss at St. John's is my dear friend in Ojai where I'm now living.

Reunion

How I Met Marvin

It was St. Patrick's Day weekend in 1981, and I was in Ojai, staying with a friend. Maggie took me to The Purple Wagon restaurant for dinner, and then we ended up at The Firebird Roadhouse to get a beer and dance. It was my first time out since my second husband had passed away. My previous experiences in Ojai had mostly taken place in the daytime. Since Ahmed and I used to entertain at home, we hardly ever went out at night, and all of a sudden, here I was meeting people that I'd only known before in the daylight.

My first encounter was with a pair of butchers that Maggie and I had known for years, and then a dentist I had gone to school with in the San Francisco Bay Area decades earlier. After that I was having a drink with a deputy sheriff. The next thing I knew, I was being shown pictures of his four children to whom he was totally devoted and of whom he was very proud; Krissi, Bryan, Suzanne, and Debbie were then—and are today—the center of his life. And I realized once again how at forty-two I really wanted to have some kids and I never wanted to leave Ojai. *Cheaper by the Dozen* was my favorite movie when I was a teenager; I'd had a child taken from me at birth and lost two other children, one shortly after he was born and one to an abortion.

As we left the restaurant, Maggie said to me, "That's Deputy Hellwitz. He's the best officer I've ever known. Whenever a lady is in distress, he's there to help her change her tire or break into her car if she's locked her keys inside."

Well, I was hooked. Marvin and I had one date and then another. Little by little as I grew to know this father, I found out he had a very mean mother who stole from him and a brother who beat up on him, and that from the beginning he had ADHD (Attention Deficit/Hyperactivity Disorder), around which he had built a way to deal with the world that worked for him nicely. Since a diagnosis of ADHD was not possible when he was a child, he had no choice but to find his own way of handling life. I often picture him climbing a Matterhorn-sized mountain every day to achieve his goals. He had earned his master's degree in public administration and was an exceptionally good detective. He enjoyed his children. Over the years, he coached endless games of soccer for their various teams. He put a roof over their heads, fed them, loved them. And as far as his children went, he always dropped everything to rush to their side if they were ever in need.

My Education Continues

When I was widowed at forty-two and found myself married to the father of four teenagers, I had a lot to learn. You would think with my background in education, nursing, and living I would have been able to handle this new job. So did I. Up until then, my world had consisted mostly of adults, and I could always go home from work at night and have my own time. This wasn't the case with four teenagers in the house.

The first morning I woke at 702 Canada Street, I got up to wake the children for school. The youngest child, Debbie, was the only one already up. We met in the front hallway and gave each other a morning hug. She looked up at me and said, "Your pits stink." Over the years Debbie turned out to be my teacher, my student. Today when I tell her she is such a good mommy, she tells me that it would never been without me.

One big change for me was I had to learn about the game of soccer and teen girls. About soccer I knew nothing;

about girls, well, I was one. In my new, ready-made, already maxed out family there were four different American Youth Soccer Association (AYSO) teams the children played on and a fifth one that Marvin coached. This meant that I, the non-soccer person, got to be the taxi driver, orange-slicer, and meal preparer for everyone before, during, and after the endless practices and weekly games so that no one went hungry. This I could do. No problem. In fact, I even had downtime when everyone was on the field. Leg warmers were especially popular at that time. Since I loved to knit, I started making them for the three girls, each on a different team.

One of the things that happens in the AYSO soccer world are weekend tournaments when teams gather from all over Southern California to compete. We also had one boy in our family, Bryan, and the boys' teams seemed to have more tournaments than the girls. This meant that the girls were expected to get up and go with us to their brother's soccer games on days when they would much rather sleep in. Their father was not inclined to leave anyone home alone. So whether their team was playing or not, everyone had to rise and shine and be in the car and ready to go at departure time. Our thirteen-year-old was the least likely to be cooperative, sleeping till the very last minute, arriving in the car still in her pj's, and getting dressed in the backseat on the way.

On one occasion, our son's team won on a Saturday and had to return for more games on Sunday. Though we were all very proud of him, we would really rather have been able to sleep in on Sunday. So I was expecting there to be three girls dressing in the back seat on the way to the game. But much to my surprise, all three girls were ready on time, each looking especially well-groomed and dressed, more like she was going on a date than going to be a spectator at a soccer game.

Silly me. I thought my suggestions and previous attempts to teach them better personal habits were paying off. I was so proud of myself and them. That is, until we reached the field and I realized that the incentive to get dressed up was really all those boys they were going to be seen by. For some reason that hadn't dawned on them the day before, but they were not going to risk a second day of humiliation because they didn't look right.

Oh, I had so much to learn from this new family of mine.

Major Rehab

When I initially met Marvin, the first stories I heard were about the children's mother. She was portrayed as a sweet alcoholic. Unfortunately, I came to learn that Marvin's first wife had some serious issues. To begin with, she would have been considered educationally handicapped in her youth had there been such designations then. She seemed to have a troubling problem of not staying home, repeatedly leaving Marvin to raise the children pretty much on his own. I would have described the family as dysfunctional, but that was how I had grown up, too, so I felt I could fix it.

About two years after we were married, a big sign appeared in town, advertising a free meeting for Adult Children of Alcoholics (ACA). The sign caught my eye because the subject applied to my newly acquired family, and I decided to attend and find out what I could do to help these children of mine grow up to be healthy and happy.

The speaker at the meeting, Bruce Gladstone, was a psychotherapist with an office in town. He slowly painted a picture of life in a family with one or more parents who drank.

As I sat listening to his presentation, I really felt for these children I was caring for. What a way to grow up! I also began to realize how this description also applied to Ahmed's three boys. Increasingly, though, I began to realize that more and more of what the speaker was saying was giving me feelings of recognition that this was how *I* grew up, too.

So it wasn't just my present four stepchildren and my previously acquired three stepsons who had a heavily drinking parent; I did too. Here I was in my mid-forties and just realizing that my dad, dead for over twenty years, had also been an alcoholic, which made me an ACA, too.

It was at the ACA meetings that I sat around a table, hearing stories quite similar to my own, but for the first time I was seeing that all the stories had the one major ingredient of alcohol. What made this so very obvious was all our stories about the fights: fights over turkeys, hams, potatoes, dressing, gravy, veggies, flaming puddings, fruit cakes, and pumpkin pies. Children crying, hiding under the big table, sitting at separate tables, or slipping out to the backyard to play when things got scary.

It was our story repeated over and over again. And we were trying to not repeat it but make it stop!

Thus I entered a twenty-year period of self-discovery through private and group therapy, books, lectures, workshops, and 12-step meetings.

Later, when I went to my mother and told her I had hep C, a disease that attacks the liver, and I could no longer drink any alcohol, she turned around and said, "Can I fix you a gin and tonic?"

"No, I can't drink that," I said. "It's alcoholic."

"Well, then would you like a beer?"

The Gift of Choices

What was the best gift ever given to me? Well, I'd have to say it was the idea that I have choices. It was the first thing I heard when I attended my first ACA lecture. Of course, the constant voice of my mother in my head at the time told me not to listen to this nonsense.

Then I was given an example of having a choice.

"Find your car keys," the speaker, Bruce Gladstone, said. "Hold them in your hand and know that any time you feel you need to leave, you can do it."

Wow! What a concept! With that knowledge I was able to relax, sit back, and listen to the rest of the presentation. That new understanding was definitely a major milestone in my life, a gift that keeps on giving. I was about forty-five years old when I heard that first presentation, and as I said, at the time my mother was still telling me what to do.

Armed with my car keys, I left that meeting with a new confidence, purpose, and goal. I was going to start making my own decisions, and one of the first had to do with money. I was beginning to realize my third husband was a poor money manager. I needed to protect what I was going to inherit from my late husband and my uncle. Unfortunately, my mother always responded to money questions with "It's none of your business!" When I'd been living with Ahmed, a man who was older than she was, she'd actively tried to disinherit me. She was convinced that he was a "bad man," who must be a communist since he was a student at UCLA; and she was certain he was after my money. How can we forget her constant refrain, "You know I don't approve of you"? I realized I had better make managing my money my business or risk losing what was coming my way, so I contacted a female broker and started developing an investment plan.

About twenty years later, I was driving Mother to see Maryann, the trust officer who handled the old family money for her. The company the trust officer worked for, originally known as the Title Insurance and Trust Co., had been founded by Mother's father, if I remember correctly. When we arrived at the parking lot, Mother told me that when we went into Maryann's office we would "not discuss" money, since it was none of Maryann business. I couldn't believe my ears.

Recently I had one of those "Aha!" moments. If I hadn't learned that I had choices, I wouldn't have been able to be responsible for those choices or for myself. How liberating is that? What personal power! What peace! Yes, I'm sorry I didn't know sooner, but I'm very grateful I finally figured it out. Choices have allowed me to take care of myself. Truly a gift of infinite value. Thank you, Bruce.

My Beautiful Child

Probably the most breathtakingly beautiful sight I have ever seen is my daughter. From her birth, when she was taken away without me being allowed to see or hold her, until she was found at age thirty, I didn't know if she was male or female, alive or dead, tall or short.

When I met my third husband, I had no idea of his exceptional abilities as a detective. I told Marvin my story and he ran with it, despite my saying the adoption should remain private according to the rules I had agreed to thirty years prior.

Then one day Marvin announced that he had found my child. She and I talked on the phone for several weeks until we felt we could arrange to meet—in a parking lot at Ventura and Van Nuys in the San Fernando Valley. After thirty years, I learned that she was a she, and that I was a grandmother as well as a mother-in-law.

From the moment I laid eyes on Mary Jane, I was totally in love, captivated by her beauty and grace. Now twenty-five years later, I am still unable to take my eyes off her when we are together.

* * *

When I first met my daughter, Mary Jane, I wanted her to know who her father was, so I went to the library and asked them to do a search on him. This is how I learned about his life. Jaime Ostos was, indeed, very famous as a bullfighter and had been written about in bullfighting literature for his creation of daring moves in the ring with the bull. Hemingway was also writing about him at around the time I met him. *Cosmopolitan* had an extensive article on him and his wife and children. There was also mention of the bulls he raised for the ring in southern Spain.

So my daughter and I learned about him together. When a friend of hers gave her a bullfighting poster, we realized that the same posters with her father's name on them were hanging on the walls of our favorite Mexican restaurant, right here in Ojai.

Soon after I met my child, my stepdaughter Debbie went to live in southern Spain for a year. While she was there, she asked around to see if she could get another poster, but was discouraged by her host family because of the matador's reputation as a womanizer. Her family said they figured he probably has dozens of children all over the world, and surely, she wouldn't want a poster with such an awful man's name on it, would she?

Now, all these years later, we have Google and don't need posters. YouTube gives us movies of this man back in his day, bullfighting. And currently he is still all over social media, being interviewed for heaven only knows what, always with a good-looking woman on his arm. Dad has been gone for over fifty years now and sometimes I wonder what he would think about how his decision played out. I got a beautiful child I love dearly, plus two grandchildren.

Juanita

After I married Marvin, my mother, Juanita, would call me all the time to say bad things about him and his children. She told me she didn't care for adopted kids or stepchildren. Then when she was here in Ojai for a visit, she and I went out to lunch with a friend of mine. In front of me, Mother told my friend that since I had never had children, I couldn't understand what they—both mothers—were talking about.

My friend almost fell out of her wheelchair.

I said I certainly *was* a mother, even though I'd had my child taken from me, and I had helped to raise seven stepchildren.

Mother said, "I don't like your friend," and left the restaurant abruptly. Needless to say, the luncheon was over.

I caught up with Mother. We walked down the Arcade to the Post Office, went back to the car, and headed home. During this walk, Mother had pretty much continued to speak negatively about my life (my marriage and my stepkids). By the time we got home, she had decided to leave, despite the fact that we had plans for dinner and she was supposed to stay for another week.

I just said, "May I help you pack?"

While we were packing her suitcase Marvin arrived and learned of what had happened. When he walked her out to her car he gave her a house key and told her, "You're welcome anytime, Juanita."

As Marvin and I watched the car's taillights fade as Mother headed down Cañada Street, I said, "You get that key back. She is not welcome in this house at this time."

When he and I went to therapy the following week, we told Bruce what had happened. He basically affirmed that I had done exactly what was needed to protect myself.

My mother and I didn't speak for three years after that. But all during that time she spoke with Marvin regularly. Now she says she likes him.

The Royal Copenhagen Mallard

I have long distance relationships with both my sisters. Over the years these relationships have ebbed and flowed but never gotten deep or strong. We have gone down very separate paths. Little Chris is a mom of three, living a hectic, stressful life in a wilderness spot in Humboldt with her highly educated husband, and Suzanne is single and travels all over the world taking pictures and writing stories for magazines like the ones you read in airplanes. She lives in plush, elegant homes in places including Santa Monica, Puerto Rico and Rancho Mirage. She is very controlling. My life has been different from theirs, with my first marriage ending in divorce after the loss of two children, and making seven moves in five years. My second marriage ended when my elderly husband died.

We had shuttled between our homes in Pacific Palisades and Ojai for about fifteen years before his death. My sole connection to my sisters is our mother, whom they care for and who for the past several years has refused to speak with me.

I have a dresser in my bedroom which acts as an altar. It holds lots of rocks and seashells, feathers and dried flowers; little statues of goddesses; a crucifix that belonged to my mom's dad; some wood from a tree in Humboldt near where Chrisy lives; some crystals; various bells; and several Egyptian artifacts, including a bust of Nefertiti, a sphinx, and some pyramids.

But what catches my eye particularly today is a small ceramic duck from Royal Copenhagen Airlines. The mallard is smooth and shiny and fits in the palm of my hand. Both wing tips are missing to one degree or another. The bird has a rust-colored bill, a green head, a white ring around its neck, and a white breast. This mallard is poised for flight.

I can still remember over fifty years ago when we were in Solvang and I got this little token of my father's love. Suzanne wanted this duck because it was Dad's favorite bird and she wanted to be his favorite girl. But that was my position as first-born, so she had to settle for a sweet plump little sparrow that she hated. There were lots of tears from her and a sense of real triumph on my part. I have carried this little duck with me now for these fifty plus years. The sense of triumph is long gone.

What I see in this little bird today is that the way I lived my life was more like Suzanne's sparrow, while Suzanne has lived the life of the mallard, flying back and forth across the country. Despite the symbolism of the birds back then, Suzanne is the one who should have had the mallard and I the sparrow.

I wonder if it's too late to give it to her. I think not.

Weddings

For me the subject of weddings is a comparative study of three events.

The first wedding was held Saturday, June 17, 1961; the second Monday, December 18, 1978; and the third Saturday, March 12, 1983. I was twenty-three, forty, and forty-five respectively. My first husband left me after five years. My second died after nine months. My third husband has decided to stay.

The location of the first was the biggest church in Hollywood. The second was a two-bed hospital room at St. John's Hospital in Santa Monica. The third was on the deck of my Uncle Jimmy's home on the beach just south of the Malibu Pier.

The guest list for the first wedding included Walt Disney and his wife, and several hundred other family members, friends, and Hollywoodites. The second list numbered four, plus the few doctors, nurses, and techs who could slip away from their duties and gather at the door of the hospital room. The third wedding was fifty-plus close friends and family, mostly from Ojai.

The first wedding was presided over by three priests: two Roman Catholic and one from the Maronite Rite of the Lebanese branch of the Catholic Church. The second was performed by a Malibu judge. The third by an Ojai Baptist minister, chosen by the groom's children.

The first wedding party had four bridesmaids and groomsmen, plus the maid of honor and best man, all in formal attire. The second only had witnesses: the bride's sister and uncle, and the groom's second son and daughter-in-law, who was carrying the groom's first grandchild. The third consisted of the groom's children—three daughters and a son—all in custom-made Sunday best.

The flowers at the first wedding were over the top, never ending. The flowers at the second consisted of a carnation for the groom's lapel and a simple cluster of pink roses for the bride's corsage. The third event's flowers were modest and included lavender flower crowns for all the girls and lovely flowering bouquets.

The first reception was held at the Beverly Hills Hotel with an ice sculpture surrounded by fresh shrimp, lobster, and crab, lots of watercress sandwiches with the crusts cut off, and French Mumm's champagne. The huge white cake decorated with gold trim had a lemon and rum filling. The second reception was created as a surprise by the hospital's president who sent a small but tasty cake from the kitchen. The bride brought in four boxes of See's Candy— chocolate-covered nuts only— for the nurses. The groom had a bottle of thirty-year-old Scotch and a ripe mango, which he shared with the family and the judge. Food for the third reception was bought at Price Club by the bride, and served by her aunt and some friends who volunteered to help out. It was a tasty buffet. The cake was decorated in lavender to match the bridesmaids' dresses. There was Cook's champagne for the adults and pink Catawba for the children and those who didn't drink alcohol.

Music at the first wedding was the organ in the church and a small strolling string ensemble at the reception. There was no music at the second wedding beyond the canned music coming from the speakers in the hall outside the hospital room. The third wedding and reception were graced with the piano talents of a friend who also helped with the buffet.

The groom at the first wedding was young and handsome and wore pinstriped pants and a morning coat with a boutonnière of orange blossoms. He was Lebanese Catholic. The groom at the wedding in the hospital was an Egyptian

Muslim in his early seventies. He wore a hospital issue cotton gown with piping at the neck and waist tie. On his robe was his boutonnière. The groom in wedding number three wore his best suit with a flower in his lapel. He was of German-Jewish ancestry, and in his forties.

The bride in all cases was the same: only her attire, age, and weight changed. Her first gown was new, expensive, and gorgeous: full-length white satin with lace at the neck and down the front. She was sporting a walking cast on her left leg and a jeweled crown on her head. Her dad walked her down the very long aisle and gave her away. Her second dress was one her first mother-in-law had given her: a pink long-sleeved wool shirtwaist dress with pink embroidered flowers down the front. There was no aisle in the hospital; no one gave her away. The third dress was cream colored, high necked, long-sleeved, tight at the waist, and short, with a full skirt. Her Uncle John walked her down the stairs and gave her away. Whatever shoes she wore at each event were not on her feet by halfway through the day's celebration.

At the first wedding, the bride and groom left the reception at the Beverly Hills Hotel in a new Chevrolet Corvair given them by the bride's father. After wedding number two, the bride drove herself home at the end of the day, and the groom stayed in the hospital to complete his radiation treatment. At the third wedding, the kids wrote all over the bride's car, a huge white Lincoln Continental with a black top. The bride and groom had to get the car washed before they could be seen anywhere. Ghosts of the paint still glowed under the fluorescent lighting at the hotel parking lot where they spent their wedding night, and the car had to be washed a second time the next day.

The honeymoon for the first marriage was one night at

the Bel-Air Hotel. The longer version was delayed due to the bride's broken ankle in a cast. There was no honeymoon for the second marriage. For the third marriage the bride and groom went to the Marriott by LAX for the wedding night, and then in the morning picked up the children from their aunt's and drove them back to Ojai for school. This time, too, the honeymoon was postponed to a later date.

So after looking at these three events in my life, how would I sum up the subject of weddings? They are all wonderful, emotion-filled, unique days in the lives of two people so in love that—no matter the details, particulars, or endings—reflect the specialness of each union. I wouldn't have missed any one of them for anything.

Three Little Words

So what do sex, money, and death have to do with each other? For me, all three were topics rarely spoken of in my family of origin. What I now know is that if you don't talk about something, explore its meaning, forms, and possible outcomes in words, then when you are faced with the reality of that subject you have no tools to deal with it. It's like being thrown into the water without having swimming lessons: some make it, some don't.

Why were both my sisters and I molested as young girls? Mother never taught us how to protect ourselves. We never learned how to say "No!" or "Stop!" Never learned to scream. Is it possible Mother was molested as a child herself and, not knowing how to protect herself, she couldn't help us?

Even though it was not talked about, money was very important in my family. We knew Dad made it by going to work so that we could have food and clothes and all of our needs met, from medicine to education to, eventually, a car for each of us. Apparently, Mom had lots of it, but Dad wouldn't let her spend any of it. It was millions, and my sisters and I knew that was a pile of money. We also knew it would come to us when she died. We knew that Mom's two brothers both lived in lovely houses on the beach in Malibu and never, ever went to work. We figured they too had millions like Mom. And we figured all those millions had come from their father and his sisters, who still lived in a mansion on Bunker Hill in downtown LA.

As the years passed and those great aunts died, the talk was that their monies had gone to Mom and her brothers. The great aunts had wanted to keep the money in the family, but they never married or had children. My sisters and I figured there had to be lots of money in those estates, and surely one day we would fall heir to it.

Time sped by, and I married and divorced and married again. Then I was widowed and married again. Chris, my youngest sister, also married and had three children. I had one child who had been adopted at birth. Our middle sister, Suzanne, became a photojournalist and never married. For a while, she took Mom around the world with her on her photo assignments, and then she moved to Puerto Rico. When Mom began to show signs of aging, our single sister decided to move back to California to help her. We married sisters offered to help, but we were assured that Suzanne had it covered. While our sister was caring for Mom, she got her to sign documents so that Suzanne ended up inheriting the bulk of Mother's estate. Christine has three children, all of whom were educated by Mother, and one of them was with Suzanne when Mother died.

He knew of the discrepancies in the settlement of the estate and asked Suzanne, "Why did you do it this way?"

Her reply was: "Your mom and Kathleen both have husbands to take care of them. I have no husband. I deserve this."

* * *

I had figured Mother's estate would be divided equally between the three of us, so when I finally learned that I was to receive a mere $15,000, I was angry, sad, and dumbfounded. What was I to do? I must admit I'd had a few plans for those savings percolating for decades in the back of my mind, and $15,000 was not going to cover them.

When I shared my story with a dear friend she simply asked me, "Did you ever really have any of that money?"

"No."

"Well, then you never really lost it, did you?"

"I guess not."

"So then, what are you going to do with the money you did receive?"

"I'm not sure."

"You could give it away."

"True." In fact, I was so irritated by the whole thing that the money had become offensive to me.

As the days passed, the idea of giving the money away to people in need who would be happy to have it really started to appeal to me. So by the time I saw my friend the following week I had decided to gift my grandmother's money for my grandchildren's college funds and give the rest to the music, art, and theater departments in the Ojai schools.

Like magic, I was happy too. I no longer felt rejected or depressed or vengeful. I felt great joy and a sense of freedom worth more than any amount of money.

It's the Tree

Marvin is such a sweet soul.

"He'd drop everything to help you," says my friend.

But what is it with him and that house? My friend and I are sitting on my front porch swing, watching my husband rake leaves into the gutter across the street.

Ever since I've been here in this house that tree in the neighbor's front yard has been a focus for him. It's a magnolia and drops its large leaves daily. Then the prevailing winds bring the leaves to our side of the street. Marvin has to rake them to keep them from coming here, or he has to go over there to get the current owners to do the job. I've hired a gardener to help him. But for him, that house may be more than just that tree. Almost fifty years ago, he moved to this neighborhood with his first wife and their young children. His boss lived across the street with his young children. For twenty years before Marvin and I met, those two families grew up together, going in and out of each other's homes and keeping an eye out for each other.

Then Marvin's wife left him for the last time. Before that, she had always left him at least twice yearly, so he had to be mother and father to his kids. Now she has full-blown dementia. When I entered the family, Marvin asked me to help him raise his kids, and I've done my best. In family therapy I learned how to help the children, but my husband was slow to change. In fact, he finally declared he didn't believe in change. So the rest of us changed around him while he held his ground. This included watching over that tree and that house.

As the house across the street sold and resold over the years, Marvin has introduced himself to each new owner and apprised them of various hidden problems, like the leak in the roof over the front door that is so hard to fix, the drainage issues, and, of course, the magnolia tree and the leaves that continue to trouble him.

Now he's seventy-seven. He has had four strokes and a lifetime of untreated ADHD. Plus, he's hard of hearing and won't get hearing aids.

So I'll just keep the gardener raking the leaves and hope the new owners don't mind this helpful neighbor too much. And I will pray Marvin can learn to let go and let the gardener do the raking.

The Meat of It

What is it about the part of the wedding vow that says "for better or for worse, in sickness or in health" that really is the meat of this relationship called marriage? When we are young and healthy we don't really appreciate the value of these words. Then comes the diagnosis and the realization that this is not going to be easy. A neighbor's husband leaves her because she is sick, and we judge him and try to help her. And we ask ourselves, "What if?" Yeah, what if?

Then it happens in our house. The multiple strokes, the Parkinson's, and nobody is themselves anymore .... Really? Actually, we are more ourselves, just different. Now we have the opportunity to really experience the meaning of those words so neatly placed in that vow. Now really, TRULY, we learn what love is, in ways we never dreamt. We grow stronger than we ever thought possible.

Gratitude

Husbands come in all shapes and sizes with all their pluses and minuses. I should know, I've had three of them. I've loved them all and appreciated each one for his special qualities and quirks. Each husband has taught me what I needed to learn while we were together. Forgiveness, gratitude, and patience come to mind. My present husband has untreated ADHD and is now dealing with the results of having had four strokes.

But through it all Marvin has continuously done something which touches my heart. When we met, he learned I had had one child taken from me at birth for adoption and I had lost another at birth. On the first occasion of my birthday with my then-new husband, he gave me a card from my son Freddie who died when he was an hour old. I cried. Marvin then gave me a card from Freddie on Halloween, Thanksgiving, Christmas, and so on.

Not many years later he used his detective skills to find my child who had been adopted at birth. Then I really cried.

Marvin continued to remember my special days with cards. Now, after having four strokes, my husband tends to forget a lot of things. So I was deeply touched when, on my latest birthday, Freddie's card awaited me at my place at the table, along with a big bunch of flowers. I'm so very moved and grateful that underneath all the frustrations of forgetting we are dealing with, that sweet, touching part of my husband still survives.

The Bird Lady

I am known in the neighborhoods where I've lived in the Ojai Valley as "the Bird Lady." When I was first married to Fred we lived in my art teacher's home in LA for a while, and he taught me to feed his favorite wild birds that came to the kitchen window each morning.

When I left LA and moved to Ojai, I continued the practice of feeding the birds in my yard. Blue jays are the most aggressive. When I'd put out a mix of seeds, all the birds would come to eat, but the jays would take all the biggest seeds first. I soon learned to hold the big seeds back and make the jays come to me for them. It didn't take long before the jays were eating out of my hand, off of my head, and even out of my mouth. I would put an unshelled peanut between my teeth and hold my hand in front of me, palm up. The jay would land on my hand and take the peanut from between my teeth.

When Marvin's kids were growing up, the school bus used to pick up the neighborhood children outside my house. Soon all the kids were hand-feeding the birds with me. Most of those kids now have their own families and have taught them to feed the birds. On occasion, we get to see one another. At those times I try to have peanuts in my purse to tuck in their hands when we meet. Yes, I still feed the birds.

Life Lessons

My Body, the Teacher

What is it with me and this body I inhabit? From the day I was born, it's been one health lesson after another. Day one I had a nosebleed, which turned into a major hemorrhage caused by a vitamin K deficiency and required three blood infusions. Not your usual welcome to this world.

For the next twenty-four years I had the usual kid stuff: measles, mumps, chicken pox, colds, flu. I had my tonsils out and wisdom teeth pulled. A normal childbirth. Then on May 1, 1962, I had placenta previa, lost the baby, and received four more blood transfusions to save my life. Little did I know then, but that was why thirty-seven years later I would be diagnosed with hepatitis C and told I had five years to live.

At that point, I was told I should do chemotherapy, but I decided to try a Chinese medicine, homeopathic, alternative medicine approach. Eat better. Exercise more. Try to stay stress free. Meditate. But I have found that every time a new challenge turns up in life, you have to face what you haven't learned yet, whatever that is. This has been especially true for me with my health.

Thirteen years later when I was diagnosed with Parkinson's, I made up my mind to face this new health lesson in the same fashion I had faced hep C. I did research and agreed to take the dopamine, increase my exercise, and eat even more plant-based food. Having been nursed from birth on canned PET milk and Karo Syrup, I'm still having lots of trouble kicking sugar. Change has been slow but sure. Then when a stroke compromised my eyesight, I gave up my driver's license and slipped into a new way of life, with rides from Little House and daily assistance from caregivers so I can keep going, enjoy my grandchildren, and pursue my art and writing classes.

Now I feel more like my Gram than ever. I have food growing in my garden. I exercise daily. Rest and tea still help. At eighty-one, I do take some meds and supplements but no pain pills or pills for depression or anxiety. I have found my brain to be my best support system. When I use it and follow my doctor's advice, I manage quite well.

I guess from day one of my life I have had to fight, and I learned early to fight *for,* not against, to be positive and grateful and satisfied and maintain my sense of humor. Pray daily. Yes, this body has taught me a lot in eighty-one years.

Thanks to all who've helped me along the way: great teachers; physical therapists; a massage therapist who knows Chinese medicine; a genius of a naturopath; an osteopath with great insight into the mind-body connection; an internist who specializes in alternative approaches and integrative medicine; a homeopathic MD; a now deceased chiropractor who did minor adjustments with major results, and who is sorely missed; another chiropractor who uses a form of biofeedback; caregivers who support my approach to wellness; a therapist who showed me how to stand up for myself; and a gifted writing teacher who is the reason I wrote this memoir. All have blessed me immeasurably.

Now I'm writing about my life and all the lessons I've learned, which seems a logical next step. And it's giving me energy. As long as God and his representatives keep collecting my tuition fee and I can afford to pay, I'll keep coming to class. I'm one lucky student.

Pursue What You Love in Life and Trust Yourself

The first thing I would say to young people is: Don't be afraid to make a mistake. Do what you like; do what you love; do what makes you feel good, because if you can do that and live the rest of your life doing that, you'll be the happiest camper on earth. Don't try to become what somebody else wants you to be: a doctor, a lawyer, a whatever. It's your decision; it's your life. Go by what your gut tells you, not by what someone else is telling you.

Unfortunately, being told how I felt was how my life started. Generally speaking, when I was born, children were best "seen and not heard," so being able to speak my mind was not acceptable. Having the notion that what I was thinking and feeling was okay wasn't acceptable. Somebody has to tell a child it is okay—a mother, father, or some other adult.

When my aunts would come to visit, I felt it was wrong of them to exclude their chauffeur from the tea we'd be having. I'd ask them, "Would Bruce like to have some tea?" "Oh, no. He's not hungry," they would tell me.

That was my first indication that something wrong was going on, because I had the sense that he was hungry, and I was being told he wasn't. I'd excuse myself to use the ladies' room and go to the kitchen and have the maid put food on a plate. I'd take it out to Bruce and he would inhale it.

It was a wake-up call for me at a very early age, which I would have to relearn later in life. I didn't carry this knowledge with me for a long time, but then I picked up on the fact that nobody else is going to be able to tell me what I'm thinking or feeling. I need to be able to do that myself. So I guess you could say that I got a late start on being me.

My Brain

I woke up this morning thinking about a lady who lived next door to my uncle at the beach in Malibu. Alice was in and out of my life from very early on; she was quiet, strong, insightful, very plain, and easy to be around. As she got towards the end of her life, I had the good fortune to be able to spend time with her. I was managing my Uncle John's care at the time, and she was caring for her husband. During this period in our lives she spoke to me of sleepless nights when she would lie in bed and pick a special day in her life and relive it. She drew strength from those memories and would rise to face each new day.

This morning I really locked in on her message to me. I'm now her age and coming to understand and value the way my mind works and how it's helping me write. Though I've been writing for decades, none of it has come to much more than boxes filled with notes. Now my mind is filled with doors, and as I open them, I find people, houses, foods, songs, and scenes that remind me of stories to tell. Much like the way the woman I knew long ago chose to remember her special days, I choose doors to open and discover the treasures of my life. And as I remember and write, I too am energized. By choosing to take writing classes, I have created a space for this to happen.

My granddaughter graduated from college last week. She now does restoration of the printed word through bookbinding. I am starting my new writing class. As we both begin our new adventures, I hope we will meet when I have a book for her to bind.

Think of It This Way

We are all victims of our own ideas. Think of it this way: If the milk is sour, we don't drink it, we throw it out. But when an idea is sour, we continue to nurse on it and then wonder why we continually feel upset or in pain.

When the battery is dead, we get a new one. But when an idea is dead, we continue to use it and wonder why we don't have the energy to get where we want to go or do what we want to do.

When there are weeds in the yard, we pull them so as to let the grass, the trees, and the plants grow and be healthy. But when we have ideas that keep us from growing to our full potential, we nurture them because they are what our parents told us. And we wonder why nothing seems to work and we feel near to death.

When are we going to learn that ideas are not sacred? They are either useful or not. And when they no longer work, it's okay to find ones that do, ones that get us where we want to go or help us be where we are in peace. When are we going to learn that what we *are* is sacred?

I Am an Artist

As I sit here looking at my one and only oil painting, I remember wanting to be an artist like Grandma Larronde, and being told I couldn't make a living with art. So I was sent to Scripps, a college that focused heavily on art, to study the humanities in preparation for being a teacher; while I was there, I wasn't allowed to take any art classes.

During my first marriage, my dear, artistic mother-in-law

took me to art classes. I loved them and did quite well. My husband Fred was very supportive. I still have and use the pencil case he gave me. During my second marriage, my husband let me draw at first. Then when he became ill, caring for him left me no time to draw. Later, during my third marriage, once the children were out and on their own, I started to take art classes again. This time I did very well with my painting and writing over a period of almost twenty years before my own health issues got in the way.

The one oil painting I did was one that my therapist encouraged me to make. It is a look inside a well that contains many of the more significant things of mine that my mother destroyed in one way or another: my ceramic handprint from grade school; my Ruthie doll; my stamp collection; the prom dress I made in my home economics sewing class that Mother turned into a clothes hamper cover; a special necklace charm a boyfriend made for me by melting down two gold bands and combining them into a larger circle with our initials joined in the middle; my Italian bikini; my child adopted away at birth; my teaching supplies; the painting of Matilija poppies I had promised my child and loaned to my mother, who then gave it away; a lovely gold leaf vase she broke; and the design I made for Adult Children of Alcoholics that she declared no one would ever buy.

It was always her way, her judgement, her decisions. Always so far above mine. There was no talking about it. "We will not talk discuss it!" was her favorite comeback.

So I painted them for all to see and talk about, if we like.

Patron of the Arts

As I sat in my wheelchair in the back of the auditorium waiting for the curtain to open on the high school spring musical, I was greeted by dear old friends, beginning with Claire, who does lighting, and James, who does sound. I saw Bill, the head of the music department, and Marty, the director. Jay, the singing coach, was at the Art Center preparing for *Macbeth*. Across the aisle from me was Janet, the new dance instructor.

Due to my Parkinson's and a recent fall, I hadn't been to the theater in quite some time, and it was wonderful to reconnect with old friends. All their hugs and thanks are such good medicine for me.

During intermission, my new caregiver told me how much she was enjoying the production. She was amazed at the outstanding quality of the performances. I told her that for the last twenty-five years I had been supporting the music and drama departments at the public elementary, junior high, and high schools in the Ojai Valley. I told her how fortunate those students are to have wonderful teachers in these departments. Their productions have always been outstanding, and many of the students have gone on in their adult lives to careers in Hollywood or on Broadway.

Up until about two years ago, my support consisted of financial donations, along with my attendance at as many performances as I was able to see. I liked going when a play first opened, then halfway through, and often again on closing night. It was fun seeing how these talented students improved over the show's run. I just wish that my health was better and I could afford to continue my financial support, but caregivers are not cheap.

On the way home, I said to my caregiver, "I guess you could say I am a patron of the arts."

Changes

What is it that's happening to me of late? I don't seem to be worried as much anymore. I've either had too much therapy, gone to too many 12-step meetings, or my Parkinson's has changed the way I think. Or maybe it was the neurofeedback? Whatever the cause, it's noticeable to me that my internal life is calmer these days. I enjoy being with friends and family, even when they have the need to go on about things that none of us have any control over. I'm especially aware that I don't feel the need to get into it with them. They are learning, too, and may not have had the same experiences I have had.

Before, I would have needed to change their minds. Now I just sit back and marvel at how each of us has our own way of problem-solving and getting on in the world. I know that each of these encounters teaches me something, and maybe one day in the future when I'm asked, I'll be able to share what I've learned and help someone in need. In the meantime, I'm listening a lot more than I used to.

Tonight at dinner as I polished off my dessert, a friend told me, "I bet you'd lick that bowl clean if you were at home."

"Sure would," I said without skipping a beat.

"I thought so," she said. "I know you!"

Yes, she does. I'm getting to know me too.

Happiness Feels Like

Happiness feels like cool, clear water all over me in a pool. My body can move effortlessly in any and all directions and I feel free. I can bend and stretch easily. I can turn and roll. I can dive deep, push off the bottom, and break through the water's surface to take a breath of fresh air. I can do the side-stroke with a scissors kick and glide. I can do the breaststroke with a frog kick that makes me lunge forward. The butterfly stroke makes me feel powerful. It's so freeing to be in the water, just floating, looking up at the sky. I love playing in the pool. It makes me feel happy, relaxed, and free. Once I swam in the dark without a suit.

When I was a teenager I didn't know what the ability to move freely was worth. Now, having Parkinson's, I understand its value is beyond measure.

Dealing with Death

When I was a young child in the late '40s, death came to my world when my Grandma Larronde became sick. She didn't come to visit anymore, and I couldn't go visit her. There was no going to see her while she was in the hospital, and then she simply wasn't there anymore. She was in heaven. In the '60s, my dad died the day after I'd visited him in the hospital. We had a funeral. I even combed his hair so he would look like my dad and not some weird stranger. Afterwards, my first husband and I took a little trip to the Santa Barbara Biltmore for several days. Then it was back to life and work.

By the late '70s, I was caring for my second husband, who was dying of cancer. Up till then, death, dying, and terminal illnesses were just not talked about. But Elizabeth Kubler-Ross was publishing her books at the time, and I was reading them while I was helping Ahmed face his death and helping his grown sons deal with the loss of their father. All the while, I was deciding that when my time came, I was not going to let any doctors experiment on me and put me through the hell I was seeing this dear man go through. I was fighting for palliative care for him long before that was an option. The doctors didn't want him to become addicted to the pain meds. I would get furious and ask, "What does it matter? He won't live long enough to get hooked. JUST MAKE HIM COMFORTABLE, FOR GOD'S SAKE!!!"

I was right there for Ahmed's death, rubbing his feet as he breathed his last, feeling his life force rush through me as he passed, while through his hospital room window I watched the entire eclipse of a full moon.

Shortly after I married my third husband in the early '80s, I helped my mother-in-law with her end-of-life issues. Then, in the early '90s, I managed my Uncle Johnny's care till his death from Alzheimer's. Soon after, I became a caring neighbor at our local Retired and Senior Volunteer Program (RSVP), sitting with people who were dying and listening to their stories, and all the while I was getting to know more and more about life and death. My own diagnoses of hep C, hypertension with irregular heartbeat, and Parkinson's came, and I now face my own end. I am looking at death and all the aspects of this phase of life, and I realize I've got to explore the issues it brings. I'm in the middle of updating my will, trust, and powers of attorney. And I'm trying to get up the nerve to ask my children what they want of mine and possibly giving it to them now.

I have decided to be as positive as possible, not do chemo, exercise daily, eat well, and do what I love: visit with my family, write, and draw. Thank God hospice with its palliative care is right down the street.

My Life

When I was growing up, my life was dictated pretty much by my folks, who had a plan that I would go to school, get a degree, get married, and get a job so I could help my husband. I was supposed to have children who I would raise and care for as they would care for me at the end of my life. Some of that happened, but not necessarily in that order.

I did go to school; I got a degree, and I kept putting one foot in front of the other, but my parents' plan kept getting away from me. Probably because it wasn't my plan. Now that I have turned eighty-one, I realize that not having a plan of my own created a rather unique life, for which I am deeply grateful and which I will continue to enjoy to the last drop. Clearly, through it all, God and my guardian angel have been ever at my side.

Thanks to those who have gone before me, including my son, my father, my second husband, and my Grandma Larronde. I am so very fortunate and grateful that my grandma taught me this about death: if you think of someone every day, then they do not really die. This truth has held me in good stead for decades. Thank you, Grandma. I know you love me, and I love you and always will. Now that I am a grandmother I know why I always wanted to be like you. This is definitely the best part, whoever's plan it was

Epilogue

Epilogue

I adore the Pacific Coast Highway. I love the way the PCH twists and turns. How it leads to places I've loved all my life. How it doesn't get to be changed often since there is no room to change it. They made a cut in the late 1800s that's pretty much stayed the same.

For me, parts of it mean where I got married.

Where my mother lived.

Where my father died.

Where my uncles surfed.

Where I found my favorite stone shaped like an egg. Then a big wave came and swept it away.

Where I saw dolphins.

Where I went to dances.

Where Gram, my mother's mother, and I picnicked, and I ate fries, burgers, and cokes before the time of plant-based diets.

Where I napped during the polio epidemic of my youth.

Where my uncles and dad caught lobsters and abalone, and I searched for pearls in the abalone guts.

Where I walked on the beach and found "real" moon-stones.

Where I held an octopus and a starfish. Cooked corn and roasted marshmallows.

* * *

Oh, this life of mine.

A solid black page with a white dot in the middle.

The PCH.

Ahmed and the desert night air off the Nile.

Chapters and chapters of romance and places and people, all peppered with the fear, anxiety, and shame of my childhood.

What did I expect when I came here to earth, to this planet? Love? Acceptance? Encouragement to be me?

What really happened? I was a vitamin-K deficient baby, so I was bleeding to death at birth. Maybe I should have paid more attention at that point. Silly me, I pushed through that non-welcome party and moved forward into my family.

When I heard or was told things I knew were not true or right, I did what I knew was. If this meant getting whipped, so be it. I learned.

I taught in Watts in the '60s. I learned.

By spending a number of years in therapy, I learned that after being raised by an alcoholic father and a fear-based mother with borderline personality disorder, I might want to make some changes in order to go forward with any degree of success or happiness.

I was raped and bore a child. I learned to say, "No!"

My genetic legacy of hypertension danced with my smoking and drinking and continuing to eat as if it were still the '50s—until hepatitis C arrived at my doorstep. So I learned about diets, exercise, supplements, acupuncture, rest, and meditation.

My mother died and I was robbed of my inheritance. I learned to make money my business.

Almost ten years later, I was diagnosed with my third fatal illness: Parkinson's. I declared this new lesson had met its match. And I learned more about diets and started new exercises.

Now that I'm officially facing death, I feel better than ever. What's to be afraid of? What am I going to get—a fourth fatal illness?

There is a flow to my life that I couldn't have had without all the experiences and illnesses and a childhood filled with fear, anxiety, and shame.

I treasure my chapters.

I have a sense of strength I've never known.

So I will be here again.

And again.

Life is sweet.

Obituary

Obituary

Kathleen Larronde Murphy Kuri El-Senoussi Hellwitz

Kathleen was born in Hollywood, CA, on June 10, 1938, to Juanita Wilkinson Larronde Murphy and William (Bill) George Murphy, Jr., at Hollywood Presbyterian Hospital. For the next twenty-three years she lived in Studio City with her parents and two younger sisters, Suzanne and Christine, their dog Fritzie, and lots of cats. During this period of her life, she attended Carpenter Avenue Grammar School and North Hollywood Jr. and Sr. High Schools. Her first two years of college were at Scripps in Claremont, CA, then she transferred to The College of the Holy Names in Oakland, CA. After her junior year, she spent the summer of 1959 traveling around Europe. Following this trip and before returning to graduate with her BA in Education, she gave birth to the child of a Spanish matador and gave the baby up for adoption.

The second period of Kathleen's life began when she met and married Frederick Emile Kuri in June, 1961. During their brief marriage they had two children, both of whom died. Fred, a member of the National Guard, was pulled out of his job in the movie industry to work at an air base in Van Nuys that was supposedly sending troops overseas to protect the Berlin Wall. In fact, the government was sending airplanes to Vietnam. During this time, Kathleen taught school in South El Monte, Watts, and Santa Monica. In the summers, she sold tickets at Disneyland. Kathleen and Fred moved seven times in five years and finally went their separate ways. While married to Fred, Kathleen began her artistic endeavors with the help of Fred's mom, also an artist.

For the next seventeen or so years, the third period of Kathleen's life, her artwork went untouched. During this time, she met and married Dr. Ahmed El-Senoussi, an Egyptian-born psychotherapist, and they lived in homes in the Pacific Palisades and Ojai with his collection of dogs and cats. Kathleen did executive secretarial work and continued to learn to cook Arabic foods. Together they completed Ahmed's research and saw him to the completion of his Ph.D. at the United States International University in San Diego. Kathleen also ran the Emotional Health Association, a nonprofit storefront psychological service, for Ahmed. They traveled to Egypt twice. They built a house in Ojai with a cantilevered swimming pool on the side of a hill, and they were Sunkist growers, specializing in pull skins, including pixies, mandarins, and tangerines. During Ahmed's long fight with cancer, Kathleen helped his sons, Helmi, Amir, and Magdi, cope with his dying.

Then came Kathleen's fourth life period. To start with, she went to work at St. John's Hospital in Santa Monica where Ahmed had died. She sold the Ojai house and moved back to the house in the Palisades, where she continued to rent out rooms as they had done when Ahmed was alive. She took her last trip to Egypt to see family and friends. Then she met Marvin Otis Hellwitz, a deputy sheriff in Ventura County, and moved in with him and his four teenage children: Krissi, Bryan, Suzanne, and Debbie. Kathleen and Marvin were married in Malibu and raised the children in Ojai, with lots of soccer practices and sliced oranges, cheerleading, carpools, sack lunches, and trips to visit relatives all over the western states. Once the children were all in high school or out in the world, Kathleen went back to her art and joyfully played at it for the rest of her life until Parkinson's got in the way. She did volunteer work for Nordhoff High School's Booster Club, ran a support group on campus for parents whose children had drug and alcohol issues, and helped out as a caring neighbor in the Hospice Program at

Little House. During this time, she also managed the care for her dear Uncle John, who had Alzheimer's. For a year, she and Marvin lived in the Bay Area, where Kathleen fed street people with the nuns from The College of the Holy Names.

After they returned to Ojai, Marvin went to work for the IRS, and Kathleen learned she had hepatitis C, acquired from a blood transfusion she received when she lost her son, Freddie, at birth. She began making lifestyle changes, including changing to a plant-based diet, exercising more, quitting smoking and drinking, and getting plenty of rest. About this time, Marvin located Kathleen's long-lost child, Mary Jane, who was living in North Hollywood with her daughter, Alcamy. Mary Jane soon remarried and moved to Tennessee with her new family, which was now increased in number by Fallon Blue, Kathleen's second granddaughter. In the meantime, Kathleen's stepdaughters, Krissi and Suzanne, both married. Suzanne married Mario Sagardoy, had two children, Kevin and Miranda, and moved to Utah. Then Debbie married Jeff Konstanzer, and they had Rowan, Devon, and Amelia while still living in Ojai before they moved to San Diego. Helmi had two children, Serena and Spencer. Serena made Kathleen a great-grandma with the birth of Seth, Madison, Solimia, and Serhiy, and later, Miranda had Jax. So all told, Kathleen had one daughter, seven stepchildren, nine grandchildren, and five great grandchildren.

In 2011, Kathleen was diagnosed with Parkinson's, and immediately applied what she had learned with her hep C to cope with this new illness. In late 2014, she started taking a new medication, Harvoni, and in early 2015, a test confirmed that she had been cleared of hep C. At the age of seventy-four, she started taking a writing workshop with Kim Maxwell and began writing her memoir.

Kathleen's passions were her family and grandchildren,

art, writing, birds, cats, cooking, flowers, music, and swimming. She tried to live her life as an example of the willingness to learn and grow with the circumstances that came her way. Her life, she came to see, was a series of lessons. She wishes to thank all those who helped support her through her final life lessons: family, friends, doctors, caregivers, teachers, and the people at Little House. She would prefer to be remembered, not missed, and cremation with her ashes scattered at sea.

"I loved this ride. It was great! Thanks!! I was blessed beyond measure."

Performance Scripts: Monologues

Thanks to Kim of Kim Maxell Studio who taught me how to write in the safest room in Ojai.

Note: I performed these monologues at Kim's studio between 2013 and 2017. Some sections from the monologues were also added to the first part of the book, and "PCH" was used as the epilogue.

Monologue #1: Famous

I wanted to be famous since before I can remember. I grew up in Studio City, California, surrounded by famous people year-round. My mother was insane for movie stars. To her, movie stars meant famous; famous meant movie stars.

Our garden was filled with clippings and slips taken after dark from the yards of our famous neighbors.

One time she pulled a U-turn in the middle of Ventura Blvd to follow Clark Gable home to get his autograph.

After a great deal of research, my mother tracked down and hired Clark Gable's maid. She actually turned out to be quite lovely. Dear Harriet was with us for decades.

My mother often confided that her deepest desire was to dance off into the sunset—with Fred Astaire.

My neighborhood was wall-to-wall movie stars. We had Audie Murphy, Mickey Rooney, and Donald O'Connor. We had Rhys Williams and George Chandler, along with regular James Dean sightings as he raced his car to and from his friend's house. Oh, and my very favorite, dear Dick Elliot with his little wiener dog. They were both so round and pleasant and fun to chat with as we walked together.

What was really fun was to see them on TV at night,

knowing they were really right next door.

Oh, and Leon Ames not only acted in movies and on stage, he owned the local Ford dealership. He was so famous he got kidnapped, stuffed in the trunk of his car, and held for ransom, making him the lead story on the nightly news, till he was found several days later.

Oh—how I longed to be famous too! But my mother's answer was always "NO."

Interwoven with famous people through carpools, school carnivals, pool parties, and Halloween. Bound by casseroles that make a neighborhood in good times and bad. And I was so close to famous, I could almost have it for breakfast. Almost.

We ate out a lot, and we always went to restaurants frequented by stars: John Wayne, Gordon McCrae, Liz Taylor—oh, the list was endless. One time, Jackie Cooper approached my parents, asking if they would bring me in for a screen test. My heart fluttered, my face flushed, and my stomach dropped to the floor.

And then, very politely, my mother said, "No."

Brushes with "my big break" would happen regularly over the years, but for however much my mother loved movie stars, her answer would forever and always be "No."

"Would your daughter like to be on the Barbara Ann Bread billboard?"

Mother: "No."

"Would your daughter like to play Grace Kelly as a young girl?"

Mother: "No."

"We're looking for a young girl to ..."

Mother: "No."

My mother would offer explanations like how she had heard that Natalie Wood was rude to a saleslady and that she didn't want me turning out that way. There were other explanations, but that was her fallback.

It's hard to know, but Mother desperately wanted to be a dancer and she married a drinker instead. Things got complicated—and then I came along. Somewhere in there, I think I got in between her and her dream of dancing off into the sunset with Fred. I think "No" was easier than "I wish you weren't here."

High school graduation led to college, and college led to jobs and husbands and relocating regularly, and the years flew by. And although fame continued to surround me, it also continued to elude me. But now I had kids, and somehow fame didn't seem to matter so much. There were classes they wanted to take and things they want to be when they grew up, so I started to address my mother's NOES by saying "YES" whenever I could. YES to art class, YES to swimming lessons, YES to cheerleading camp, soccer teams, lessons, trips, classes. Yes. Yes. Yes.

YES turned out to be more fun than I anticipated. So when my kids left home, I started saying YES to other kids. Donating to arts organizations that give kids a voice. Those YESES led to me taking up residency in the front row of a little hole-in-the-wall theater to witness those young voices take flight. I ended up liking the front row so much I stayed to watch all the other voices of that little theater come to life. Plays and concerts and poetry— they called it "theater in your lap"—and I went there a lot. The front row of Theater 150 became my second home.

Then like all good things, it changed, and so did I. Mostly I got older. Trips to Starr Market, Little House, the bank, and Rainbow Bridge were followed by more trips to Starr Market, Little House, the bank, and Rainbow Bridge.

And then one day—I heard it.

"It's you! Front Row Lady. You're the Front Row Lady from Theater 150!"

It was one of the sweet young voices I had watched take flight many times from my front row seat.

"Seeing your face at every show—changed my life. I love you."

She was clasping my hands in hers.

We hugged and laughed and swapped stories, and she was on her way. And I stood there in the vitamin aisle, motionless.

Oh my, it had finally happened. After all this time. I was Front Row Lady. I was famous.

Oh my. Being famous is so much sweeter than I had imagined.

Monologue #2: Black and White

About twenty-four miles from Studio City where I grew up is Compton Avenue Elementary School on 104th Street in Watts. A few blocks east of the Harbor Freeway, the school is directly in the flight path for Los Angeles International Airport.

It is August, 1963. I'm going for an interview for my first teaching position. Bright light is reflecting off bare house walls, almost blinding me. Roofs mostly flat. Grass sparse. Trees few and far between. It's warm.

I pull up to the curb and notice several men gathered in front of the housing project across the street. They stop talking and watch this freshly graduated, newly married, and obviously white girl get out of her car and walk into the school.

I am greeted by Juanita, Mr. Thompson's lovely, loyal, and all-knowing secretary. Mr. Thompson may be the principal, but it's obvious Juanita really runs the school.

Impressed that I actually got out of my car, Mr. Thompson hires me on the spot.

Instead of an interview, Juanita leads me down the hall to where my kindergarten room awaits. My brain is packed with songs and games for my new eager little learners, and my closet at home is full of red shoes.

Kindergarteners love bright colors, and my shoes are perfect!!!

As we walk, Juanita lets me know that since there weren't enough children to make up a kindergarten class AND since the 5th grade transfer teacher from Vermont DIDN'T get out of her car, I will be teaching 5th grade.

I try not to panic as Juanita leaves me to prep my room with a few words of advice:

DON'T smile for at least a month if you want to have any order or control. AND if you wish to maintain possession of your purse and school supplies, LOCK the door every time you leave.

I stand alone in my new classroom with no lesson plans, the wrong shoes, and the overwhelming realization that they hadn't covered any of this in college.

My first day is crazy with noise and a blur of students taller than me. Several of them belonged in junior high, but had been held back. I can't help but feel a little like Dorothy in a pair of embarrassingly inappropriate red shoes. This was not the first day I had prepared for or dreamed of.

At the height of all the confusion, Mr. Devereaux, the Special Ed teacher from the room next door, appears unexpectedly: a professional football player turned teacher with a refrigerator-sized body that fills my doorway.

"If you need any help, Mrs. Kuri, you know where my

room is." An echo of his powerful voice fills the room, and a hush of respect for this gentle giant settles over my class. He gives them one last look as he turns to leave. My Guardian Angel has saved the day.

"Thank you, Mr. Devereaux. Thank you so very much."

It is now fall of 1963, and although the Civil Rights Movement has begun, there are no laws written or signed to support the kind of equality needed for integration. This means that no matter who you are, where you come from, or how much you make, Watts is the first place you live if you are black and moving to L.A. You are not going to be welcomed into white neighborhoods, and your children are not going to be welcomed into white schools. Watts is a must stop and often a permanent one.

As the weeks pass, I get to know my students better and better. Most of my parent-teacher conferences are held in the home.

Denise is a fashionably coiffed and well-dressed little girl, smart as a whip. Her home is surrounded by a lovely green lawn with landscaped flowers and shrubs. It is by far the nicest house on the street. Draperies left open reveal a beautifully furnished living room.

Ivory lives next door to Denise and is a very tall boy. Polite, shy, and quiet, he struggles with math. His home has a single tree by the curb, probably planted by the city. No curtains or shades. The front window reveals a bare wood floor with a mattress, TV, and a small diapered child eating from a jar of peanut butter.

James is a tight ball of energy. Smart. Witty. Quick. Not inclined to sit and do his lessons. His big black eyes glisten with long lashes. He has a great smile and is a real pain in the neck. I don't know whether to punish him or laugh, and he knows it. Since James has no address on file, I don't think he has a real home.

Denise's mother is an escort.

Ivory's father is a minister.

And James, well, I never met his parents.

* * *

"We're gonna sell more candy bars than you!!"

These words ring through the halls of Compton Avenue Elementary School. The fall fundraiser is upon us, and, boy, is it a contest! Each student is sent home with order forms to entice their family and friends into buying the sweet, nutty confections.

Your teacher, unrecognizably disguised as a witch, is the Grand Prize every student longs for.

After leading the Halloween parade, and after an unimaginable amount of suspense, the disguised teacher will rip off the mask, revealing the winner to the screaming delight of the entire school. Driven to see me dressed as a witch, my class sells and sells and sells chocolate bars. Until one day Juanita informs me that my class has won, and it is time for me to go buy yards and yards and yards of black crepe, black tights, long striped socks, a long-sleeved black turtleneck, black gloves, a scarf, a pointy hat, and a mask to disguise my incredible whiteness.

Well, it's the day of the parade, and Juanita has pulled all the right front office strings to buy me the time I need to make my transformation.

She also successfully helps me stuff and fold and cover every inch of me, so when I'm dressed none of the white me shows.

This is it—the witching hour! I confidently march onto the crowded playground. I lead the whole student body past the judges' platform. Success! No one knows it's me. James, my beautiful pain-in-the-neck ball of energy, is being held in tow by Mr. Thompson, the principal. I take my place beside them as the students start to settle for the big moment.

Then I hear James trying to contain himself. "Mr. Thompson, Mr. Thompson. We won—my class won!"

I hear Mr. Thompson respond calmly, "James, what would make you think that?"

James replies with his trademark smile, "Because the witch is pigeon-toed—and so is Mrs. Kuri."

Barely able to contain my laughter, I unmask myself, and all my students go wild. Screaming and backslapping follows as they rush in around me. James bellows that he knew all along the witch was me. I am so proud. AND pigeon-toed, apparently.

As the excitement of the victory winds down, Denise takes my hand, and we walk around the playground, enjoying all the day has brought.

A little girl from another class walks up to us and asks Denise, "Is this your mom?"

I can barely breathe.

The world stops for just a moment.

It is so profoundly beautiful.

This is what it looks like to be color-blind.

This is what it feels like.

I stand motionless and humbled, not sure which of us is the teacher.

Monologue #3: This Life of Mine

SING: THE BROWNIE SONG

Chapter I: The Ice Queen

We called my mother the Ice Queen.

When we were old enough to be curious about how we got here, my sister and I asked her, and she took out a book called *Being Born* and showed us a picture at the front of the book: a solid black page with a white dot in the middle. Under the picture it read, "This is how we all began."

Wow! Our interest was certainly piqued!

So we asked just how we got from that dot to us ...

Aaannd she closed the book and said, "Go ask your father."

Thus our sex education was taken over by an Irish alcoholic who:

Fancied himself quite the ladies' man,

Needed to tell us all his stories about his conquests,

AND ...

Wanted his daughters to be virgins when they married.

Which is why MY sex ed became a learning-by-doing experience.

Chapter II: PCH

I adore the Pacific Coast Highway. I love the way the PCH twists and turns. How it leads to places I've loved all my life. How it doesn't get to be changed often since there is no room to change it. They made a cut in the mountains in the late 1800s that's pretty much stayed the same.

For me, parts of it mean where I got married.

Where my mother lived.

Where my father died.

Where my uncles surfed.

Where I found my favorite stone shaped like an egg. Then a big wave came and swept it away.

Where I saw dolphins.

Where I went to dances.

Where Gram, my mother's mother, and I picnicked, and I ate fries, burgers, and cokes before the time of plant-based diets.

Where I napped during the polio epidemic of my youth.

Where my uncles and dad caught lobsters and abalone, and I searched for pearls in the abalone guts.

Where I walked on the beach and found "real" moonstones.

Where I held an octopus and a starfish. Cooked corn and roasted marshmallows.

I love PCH.

CHAPTER III: Ahmed Loved to Dance

Oh! How Ahmed loved to dance! Especially to Latin music. How strong his arms were. What fun it was.

Along with dancing in the living room, he told me stories of dancing in the nightspots in Cairo and Alexandria, with King Faruk at ringside.

The lovely night air off the Nile.

The sweet smell of flowers from the street vendors.

The magic of it all in the words he used to tell of his memories.

And then it was the two of us dancing in those romantic locations for real, and it was more magical than I'd imagined it would be.

I'm so lucky now to have those firsthand memories of my own. They make for very sweet dreams now that I am older than he was. You were right, Ahmed. God does provide.

EPILOGUE

Oh, this life of mine.

A solid black page with a white dot in the middle.

PCH.

Ahmed ... and the desert night air off the Nile.

Chapters and chapters of romance and places and people, all peppered with the fear, anxiety, and shame of my childhood.

What did I expect when I came here? Love? Acceptance? Encouragement to be me? What really happened? I was a vitamin-K deficient baby, so I was bleeding at birth. Maybe I should have paid more attention at that point. Silly me. I pushed through that non-welcome party and moved forward into my family.

When I heard or was told things I knew were not true or right, I did what I knew was. If this meant getting whipped, so be it ... I LEARNED.

I taught in Watts in the '60s ... I LEARNED.

By spending a number of years in therapy, I LEARNED that after being raised by an alcoholic father and a fear-based mother with borderline personality disorder, I might want to make some changes in order to go forward with any degree of success or happiness.

I was raped and bore a child. I LEARNED to say, "No!"

My genetic legacy of hypertension danced with my smoking and drinking and continuing to eat as if it were still the '50s—until hep C arrived at my doorstep. So I LEARNED about diets, exercise, supplements, acupuncture, rest, and meditation.

My mother died, and I was robbed of my inheritance. I LEARNED to make money my business.

Almost ten years later, I was diagnosed with my third fatal illness, Parkinson's. I declared this new lesson had met its match. And I LEARNED more about diets and new exercises.

Now that I'm officially facing death,

I feel better than ever. What am I going to get—a fourth fatal illness?

COME ON!!!

There is a flow to my life that I couldn't have had without all the experiences and illnesses and a childhood filled with fear, anxiety, and shame.

I treasure my CHAPTERS.

I treasure standing up here all alone in front of you, reading them aloud. There is something so special about this exchange.

I have a sense of strength I've never known.

So I will be here again.

And again.

Life is sweet.

SING: THE BROWNIE SONG

Monologue #4: Approval

"Well, you know I don't approve of you." That was one of my mother's favorite sayings.

So you may be wondering what I am doing wearing a blue bikini and drinking out of the carton in my fridge. Where did this behavior come from? Certainly I was raised to know better.

Well, it kind of started with the sweet, creamy gelato I'm bringing home from Rainbow Bridge these days. One day I decided to forgo using a dish and started eating directly from the container. I figured maybe I'd eat less. I can't say for sure one way or the other. What I do know for sure is that it's been a slippery slope to drinking this Perfectly Protein Mocha Cappuccino right out of the carton in my fridge.

It's not like I'm a zombie and eating brains or anything—but it is kind of gross.

"Well, you know I don't approve of you."

It's 1959 and I am twenty-one and walking down the street in Rome with two girls on my European student tour. We are being followed by three Italian boys who are practicing their English. We are each looking for a bathing suit. The hotel suits are way too pricey. So eventually we let these three eager fellows lead us to an Italian store with wooden tables piled high with clothes—including swimsuits.

After much trying ... and giggling ... and staring, we each bought a suit.

I got a blue bikini.

I liked the way it fit.

Then, it was early evening at our next stop on the tour.

There were no sandy beaches nearby, just concrete walls with metal ladders leading down from the promenade, which was filling with early evening strollers. I waded out into the Mediterranean Sea in my new suit, attracting a bit of a crowd.

I think they thought I was someone famous.

It was silly—and kind of magical.

When I returned home, my mother threw my bikini away.

"Well, you know I don't approve of you."

Ahhh, the soundtrack that has underscored my life.

Sometimes soft and cautious, sometimes loud and penetrating.

"Well, You Know I Don't Approve of You" was originally composed and performed by my mother, but it has been covered by many artists, including all three husbands, several teachers, a couple of bosses, and a well-intended friend or two.

I'm pretty sure I've hummed a couple of bars of it myself.

"Well, you know I don't approve of you."

I'm not sure what's been happening to me of late. I don't seem to be worried as much anymore. I've either had too much therapy, gone to too many 12-step meetings, or my Parkinson's has shaken my self-consciousness out of me.

I don't know, but I'm thinking of replacing the old soundtrack with something like ...

"Hi, gorgeous. I love you and appreciate you."

or

"Hey, beautiful. Thanks for always having my favorite food in the fridge."

or

"My dear sweet soul mate, you look like someone famous in that blue bikini. You should probably drink that Perfectly Protein Mocha Cappuccino directly out of the carton, and then put it right back in the fridge."

"Well, you know I don't approve of you."

Yes, Mother ... and a variety of other critics. I know you don't approve.

It's just that ... I don't give a flying fuck!!!

Which is not to be confused with "I don't care" or "I'm just being lazy."

LET'S CREATE SOME PERSPECTIVE HERE!

1. No one else in the house drinks it.

2. I'm not hurting anyone.

3. When my daughter comes to visit, I'll get out a glass

... and probably put on some pants.

In the meantime,

I'm going to stand right here in front of my fridge,

inside of MY house,

in MY blue bikini ...

and celebrate MY victory over oppression!

I may even hug myself.

Kathleen Hellwitz drinks from the carton in the fridge, ladies and gentlemen.

Yes.

She does.

Talk amongst yourselves ... if you wish.

Monologue #5: Bunker Hill to Bird Lady

"Some of these days you're gonna miss me, honey ...
Some of these days you'll feel so lonely ...
You'll miss my huggin' ... You'll miss my kissin' ...
You'll miss me, honey, when you go away ...
I feel so lonely. Just for you only ...
You know you have had your way ...
And when you leave me, I know you'll grieve me ...
You'll miss your little daddy ...
Some of these days."

As a young child I was always threatening my sweet, loving father that I was going to run away from home, and he got me every time by singing, "Some of These Days" and getting me to tearfully relent.

Memories of visiting the family mansion on Bunker Hill in

downtown Los Angeles overlap with memories my borderline personality disorder, celebrity-obsessed mother and my alcoholic, traveling salesman, Irish father.

There are piano recitals ... gone bad. Elementary school piano recitals, also a disaster, followed by tears. Tears and then more tears for my butchered hair, successfully shoved under my high school graduation cap after a nip of sherry.

There was college and then Spain and being raped and having my child adopted away; followed by secrets and teaching elementary school in Watts; and driving across the Bay Bridge on a rainy evening when the Angels beat the Giants when I ended up in the trunk of the car ahead of me with the steering wheel in my gut and a broken ankle.

There's an "unfortunate selection" of a first husband, a "romance to end all romances" of a second husband, and ... a "Well, I never thought I'd get lucky for the third time" of a husband who found my child who'd been adopted away thirty years earlier. There were stitches and casts and marriages and a ... substantial inheritance lost to a broken, angry, and lonely sister.

There are eight kids, nine grand kids, and four greats.

Then came the moves. First, east of the greater Los Angeles area to El Monte, San Gabriel, and Alhambra. And then back west to LA, Brentwood, Santa Monica, and Pacific Palisades. And finally to Ojai, to a lovely house where we grew mandarins for Sunkist, and then another lovely house and feeding birds with the children of children I fed the birds with years and years before.

I have been:

- *Daughter*
- *Student*
- *Teacher*
- *Wife*

- *Mom*
- *Widow*
- *Artist*
- *The Bird Lady*
- *Have-a-Cookie-and-Juice-at-the-Bus-Stop Lady*
- *Front Row Lady*
- *Patron*
- *Neighbor*
- *Friend*

I have been mistaken for a nun by the beautiful homeless people I served in the soup kitchen in downtown Oakland behind the city jail.

Parkinson's, acupuncture, homeopathics and hepatitis C; massage and hypertension, prayer, A-fib like Arnold Palmer, and keeping the candle lit; restless legs, patience and a 60th reunion ... Doing laundry, laundry, and more laundry. And exercise followed by more and more exercise. And of course music and more music ... and how I love to write.

There have been thoughts, thoughts, lots of thoughts of ridding the world of things painful, things fearful, things hurtful. Yet each time one comes to mind I realize that it has a reason to be here. Each has a lesson to teach. And without those lessons we could never learn all life has to teach. So as much as I would like to abolish Parkinson's and cancer, war and death, thoughtless or harmful behavior, and natural disasters, I think each has a value. A way to teach us that no other has.

I think we ultimately need the patience, compassion, acceptance, understanding, forgiveness, and humility these challenges bring, which allow us to be grateful for the positive aspects of life. Here is where years of meditation pay off. Learning to let go and allow judgment, fear of change, needing to be right, needing to control, and the desire for vengeance slip away to make room for the learning.

And to find the ever-elusive inner peace we all crave. Above all, I know I'm never too old to learn.

"Some of these days you're gonna miss me, honey ...
Some of these days you'll feel so lonely ...
You'll miss my huggin' ... You'll miss my kissin' ...
You'll miss me, honey, when you go away ...
I feel so lonely. Just for you only ...
You know you have had your way ...
And when you leave me, I know you'll grieve me ...
You'll miss your little daddy ...
Some of these days."

Monologue #6: The Morning After

When Carrows closed, I wasn't the only one who was saddened. Not because I'd miss the food, certainly, but the waitresses were not just long-standing friends, but more like family: Candy, Cindy, Rosa, and Marisal. And who could forget Lauren? Who, if she liked you, would always give you two scoops, not just one, in your small sundae ... with extra chocolate sauce and whipped cream. Oh! You NEVER wanted her to not like you.

My grandchildren always enjoyed the meals we had there on "kids' night," complete with face painting and balloon animals. And the placemats they loved to color and play games on.

Now it's called Beacon Coffee—and I love the place. They use the Chemex coffee maker I grew up with and hadn't seen in decades. Plus, they make sesame brittle to die for. The coffee is good, too.

On Friday, I took my daughter there for a treat. Little did I know I'd be the one to get the treat. As we sat enjoying ourselves, an elderly gentleman asked if he could share our table. This happens a lot at Beacon. Of course we welcomed him.

As we made our introductions, I learned his name was George. But my ear told me this man was probably from the Middle East. Having spent over 20 years in that world myself with my first and second husbands, my ear recognized the familiar lilt I hadn't heard in far too long.

Sure enough, George was born in Alexandria, Egypt ... one year before me!

George lives in Canada now. He has been an ambassador between governments over many, many years.

As we shared our respective stories, it became amazingly unbelievable just how many Egyptians we both have known, how many places we have in common, and how many times our lives could have intersected.

My late husband was an Egyptian who practiced psychotherapy in the Middle East as well as in the United States. Before coming to the States, he had counseled King Faruk and presidents Nasser and Sadat. When we traveled back to his roots, we often met and dined with members of the Egyptian Parliament and other government officials who had been imprisoned by Nasser. Out of respect for one another and all they had endured, they still called each other by the prison numbers they were required to use there instead of their given names.

At this point, George and I spoke of our concern for our beloved Egypt, currently going through some very rough waters. And George expressed his concern for us in our current electoral cycle.

George just happened to be in Ojai with his daughter, who was doing some business with a friend, and he had decided to stop in at Beacon for a light snack and some coffee while his daughter worked. It was definitely a comfort for him to find a place at a table with people who had such an unexpected connection to him. We shared our sesame brittle with him and spoke at length:

About Middle Eastern food, especially the spices we so enjoy ...

Famous landmarks ...

Ancient architecture ...

Our favorite belly dancers ...

And, of course, our grandchildren.

And then we exchanged email addresses and—as quickly as we had met—we parted ways.

Who knows if or when we will enjoy another special moment like that?

November 9, 2016. The morning after ...

When I first heard it, I said to myself, "I will NEVER watch the news again."

Several of my neighbors who regularly walk past my house with their dogs were in tears at five and six in the morning over their Medicare, their Social Security, who their daughter would live with when they got deported, or whether their marriage would be invalidated. What that would this mean to the love of their life?

I gave the dogs their usual biscuits and tried to encourage their owners to keep going on their walk—and maybe let the dust settle before making themselves sick with worry.

Then I realized that their walk would most likely be significantly longer than mine.

My beautiful friends and neighbors, for that I am truly sorry.

Be kind with yourselves.
Be kind to those around you.
And do the best you can, especially now, to make room at your table for o
thers.

Monologue #7: Itsybitsypray

Brothers and sisters of the front row and beyond, I stand before you today with expectations hovering above my head, expectations of what is possible in a day—or a lifetime.

Brothers and sisters, please fold your hands, but do not close your eyes.

Never close your eyes.

(Dramatic reading)

Ohhhhhhhhhhhh,
The itsy-bitsy spider climbed up the waterspout.
Down came the rain and washed the spider out.
Out came the sun and dried up all the rain,
And the itsy-bitsy spider climbed up the spout again.

When I wake each day, I do a check of my body.
Yes, I do.
It lets me know I need to pee, and without a second thought, I find myself in the bathroom.

Hallelujah!

I find myself in the middle of my morning routine:

prayers, core strengthening exercises, brain training, sensible food, and more meds than any great-grandma could possibly shake a stick at. They are the glue and the Band-Aids that help me make it through my day in one piece.

Hallelujah!

I have trouble making my fingers work. It's not like I've forgotten; it's my body that can't remember. It may take longer than I would like, but I get a lot done by the end of my day.

My heart and spirit have not forgotten how to keep trying.

Hallelujah!

I have given up news—for music.

Harsh words—for softer ones. And, doing everything on my own—for asking for help.

Hallelujah!

Oh, but brothers and sisters, some days a great-grandma falls short of the mark.

Some days great-grandma forgets that her dear, totally-devoted-to-his-family spouse has lost a good portion of the reasoning part of his brain to four strokes and an ADHD-challenged childhood. Some days I am not so great.

Hallelujah!

Some days my need to have a person who hears me and understands me runs headlong into his need to be with someone who does the same for him. Instead of someone who can be impatient and angry and frustrated at times.

Hallelujah!

Some days I forget St. Patrick's Day, 1981, in Ojai, California, when my friend took me to The Purple Wagon for dinner and The Firebird to dance, where I had a Heineken's with a deputy sheriff who carried dozens of pictures of his four children with him everywhere.

I forget the day he located the child I was forced to give up at birth.

And the kitchen we remodeled,

And the hot tub we put in,

Only sixteen years later to give it away on Craig's List.

I forget the years he spent visiting his mom daily in an Ojai rest home with me at his side.

Hallelujah!

He turned out to be exactly as my friend had described that night in Ojai in 1981: a Deputy Sheriff who was really good at being right where you needed him, right when you needed him the most.

Hallelujah!

Thirty-five years later: eight kids, nine grandkids, and five great grandkids; and births and deaths, graduations and weddings, soccer games, vacations, and Girl Scout Cookies; and he is a Republican, and I am a Democrat.

Hallelujah!

My Parkinson's, hypertension, and restless legs collide with his stroke damage, ADHD-challenged childhood, and fender benders on repeat.

Hallelujah!

Oh yeah, though I walk through the valley ...
For better or for worse,
In sickness and in health ...

Is this what it feels like to be given the opportunity to really experience the meaning of those words so neatly placed into vows made so long ago? Those words are so much messier now, mixed with behavior, diagnosis, reality.

Is this how true love plays out?

At times I wonder at how my life has turned out. Not at all the way I planned it when I was young: a big house like Grandma's, lots of children like in *Cheaper by the Dozen*, and no serious problems. Just a successful family with everyone fulfilling their dreams.

Hallelujah!

Brothers and sisters, my life looks nothing like that at all.
It is a big, messy, high-maintenance life
Filled with complications, illness, and schedules ...
And humor and friends.
And romance, adventure, and memories.
And the memories mix with the mess ...

And maybe I didn't get what I wanted.
Maybe I got what I needed.

Maybe we have grown stronger than we ever thought imaginable.
Maybe my life would have been boring and dull and ...

Hallelujah!
Brothers and sisters of the front row and beyond, please open your program to the
"Itsy-Bitsy Spider." Call and response and ...

KATHLEEN:
Oh, the itsy-bitsy spider climbed up the waterspout.

BROTHERS AND SISTERS:
Down came the rain and washed the spider out.

KATHLEEN:
Out came the sun and dried up all the rain.

EVERYONE:
And the itsy-bitsy spider climbed up the spout again.

AMEN

And Finally . . .

Thank you to my granddaughter Alcamy for those copies of the book she hand-bound for the family.

Thank you to dearest Irene for being my eyes through this adventure of writing a memoir.

Thank you to my editor, Stephanie Quinn Westphal, without whom this book would not have happened.

LOVE • LIGHT • PEACE

Lightning Source UK Ltd.
Milton Keynes UK
UKHW031232040220
358138UK00009B/1314